# *Folk Tales on* *The* SETTLE-CARLISLE RAILWAY

# *Folk Tales on*
# *The*
# SETTLE-CARLISLE RAILWAY

W. R. Mitchell MBE

FONTHILL

*Dedicated to Peter Fox, my long-term friend and railway enthusiast, who also provided a number of pictures for this book.*

Fonthill Media Language Policy

Fonthill Media publishes in the international English language market. One language edition is published worldwide. As there are minor differences in spelling and presentation, especially with regard to American English and British English, a policy is necessary to define which form of English to use. The Fonthill Policy is to use the form of English native to the author. W. R. Mitchell was born and educated in Skipton, North Yorkshire and now lives in Giggleswick, North Yorkshire; therefore British English has been adopted in this publication.

Fonthill Media Limited
Fonthill Media LLC
www.fonthillmedia.com
office@fonthillmedia.com

First published in the United Kingdom
and the United States of America 2015

British Library Cataloguing in Publication Data:
A catalogue record for this book is available from the British Library



ISBN 978-1-78155-321-3



Typeset in 10.5pt on 13pt Sabon
Printed and bound by CPI Group (UK) Ltd, Croydon, CR0 4YY

# CONTENTS

1

# Up Hill, Down Dale: A Spectacular Railway

The Settle–Carlisle, one of the great Victorian railways, began in the heart of England. Barge-owners who transported coal by canal sought a share in the rail traffic that rival companies were operating between England and Scotland. Efforts in the 1850s to join up with the London and North Western railway failed. Shrewdly, the Midland decided to occupy a central route, absorbing a project that extended to Hawes. The main interest was in Scottish traffic. Despite hilly terrain, the Midland created a fast, all-weather rail link between Settle and Carlisle, crossing a watershed.

A Parliamentary Act granted a strip of land to the young and thrustful Midland company, with a length of 72 miles (1,728 yards); the Hawes branch had a length of 6 miles (132 yards). It was left to the company's valuers to acquire land through negotiations with the owners. James Farrer, of Ingleborough Estate, possessed land that embraced Blea Moor and Gearstones. He had opposed the Settle–Carlisle bill in 1866, but now he benefited hugely. A huge viaduct would be constructed on an area known as Batty Moss.

James Allport, the Midland's general manager from 1860 until 1880, observed, in a reflective mood: 'If I had one work in my life that gave me more anxiety than another, it was the Settle–Carlisle line.' He and John Crossley, the chief engineer (who had delayed his retirement), toured the strip of land concerned. He was the man who would design and supervise the construction of bridges and viaducts.

We tend to think of the line as being built by brawny navvies, yet each contractor had agents, engineers, sub-contractors, clerks, inspectors, and cashiers. Specialisation was necessary. In the large workforce were brickmakers, carpenters, cement-burners, engine-tenters, firemen, gangers, horse-keepers, masons, mechanics, miners, mortar-grinders, saddlers, sawyers, and time-keepers.

The Settle–Carlisle project, extending to 86.8 miles between Skipton and Carlisle, was to be a considerable drain on financial resources. A railway that would cost the Midland Company £3.6 million—50 per cent above the estimate—sprang from inter-company rivalry between them and the London and North Western Railway. The route was to take in north-south sections of two pastoral dales—North Ribblesdale and the Eden Valley. Pennine fells would form a dramatic backdrop. Tracts of moorland and rough pastureland were speckled with horned sheep. Villages and farms were linked with walls made of local stone, without a dab of mortar.

The Midland devised what would be the last important railway in the land to be built using the traditional pick-and-shovel method. The efforts of around 6,000 navvies would be involved. The ceremony of cutting the first sod took place in November 1969. The permanent way would consist of 82-lb steel rails; block-signalling apparatus and interlocking points and levels would enable the Settle–Carlisle to cope with heavy traffic moving at high speed.

The most arduous stretch would lie between Blea Moor and Ais Gill. For 10 miles the line would traverse what Camden, an old-time topographer, had described as 'a horrid silent wilderness'. In contrast were the light-grey limestone scenery of North Ribblesdale and the New Red Sandstone of the Eden Valley. The Settle–Carlisle railway climbed so steeply—1 in 100 from Settle up to about Ais Gill—that this stretch became known as The Long Drag.

In the days of steam, firemen worked hard to keep the loco fire glowing and the steam pressure high. The first express train of this new service left St Pancras, London, at 10.30 a.m. on 1 May 1876, and in due course a hundred or more trains a day were beating a rhythm on the steel rails. The Midland had the services of Kirtley, a brilliant engineer who devised railway locomotives. However, they proved rather small; driver and fireman had little protection against the weather.

The Settle–Carlisle would be thrashed during the two world wars when it conveyed troops and vital equipment. A number of bridges were strengthened to allow for the movement of heavier locomotives. After the First World War, and onwards to the end of the steam period, there appeared on the lines a bewildering but fascinating variety of locomotives.

My interest in the history and traditions of the Settle–Carlisle Railway began around sixty years ago. Most of the tales I heard of the steam-train period came from railmen who had worked on footplates, with the glow of fire and clatter of coal. One of many amusing tales related to a cricket match that took place at Settle, on land adjacent to the railway; a batsman clouted a ball that landed on a passing goods train, and was it borne for 72 miles, being taken out at Carlisle.

T. P. Brown, the deputy coroner, conducted many inquests, which in due course were held at inns, including the Welcome Home at Batty Green. James Mathers, its host, died at Ingleton; he tumbled when trying to stop his runaway horse. A wagon wheel ran over him. There was a hostelry called 'Pavilion' at Dent Head. During the construction period of the line, a police superintendent based at Settle investigated complaints about the illicit local sale of beer and spirits. He was determined to put a stop to it, believing that the ale-can was responsible for most of the local crimes.

David Page, Medical Officer of Health for Sedbergh, was concerned at the 'state of puddle' on land around shanty huts at Dent Head, where railway workers and their families resided. Surface water and refuse were being thrown out immediately from the doorways. Page was also concerned at the workmen's living quarters—they were over-crowded. In one hut he found that five bedsteads were jammed so tightly together that the sleepers on the furthest bed had to clamber over several others to reach it.

O. S. Nock, a railway historian, knew the railway line since his boyhood, having attended Giggleswick School. Ozzie (as he was known, though not always to his face) recalled for me with pleasure the exhilaration he had felt when crossing Dent Head Viaduct and travelling through Rise Hill tunnel, 'out once again on that dizzy ledge above Garsdale to the highest water troughs in England'.

There were to be Royal occasions. Queen Elizabeth, mother of the present Queen, joined a Royal Train overnight at Dent station.

A local policeman stood on the bridge near Salt Lake. Men were stationed at the head of every tunnel shaft on Blea Moor and at Ribblehead Viaduct. Not long before the arrival of the Royal train, some cows had been taken off a pick-up train and driven into a lineside pen so that they would be 'ready for t'farmers next morning'. The cows broke out of their pen and wandered down the line towards Salt Lake. A railman recalled, 'We had to run after them and get 'em back ... We managed it just before t'Royal Train came along.'

Settle station, constructed in Victorian times, had some exterior recesses on its façade. Two of them held effigies of Mickey and Minnie Mouse. The former had been found tacked to a highpoint of a telegraph post at Dent station in the winter of 1947. A railwayman, noticing the effigy partway up the side of an enormous snow-drift, was able to recover it. Set in another recess is Minnie Mouse, another Walt Disney creation. When Yorkshire breezes stripped early models of her clothing, its place was taken by a bottle with a Minnie-like appearance.

In a waiting room at Settle is a memorial to Alfred Wainwright, the celebrated fell-walker. He had undertaken from this station a long-distance walk along a route that was taken into account when he devised what became the celebrated Coast to Coast Walk. A plaque affixed to a wall at Appleby station strikes a sad note in the heart of anyone who reads the words, for the inscription commemorates Eric Treacy, former Bishop of Wakefield, and prime walker. He collapsed and died at the station on 13 May 1978.

Millions of words have been written about the course taken by the Settle–Carlisle railway. A writer in the *Carlisle Patriot* referred to the central part of the route as:

> ...a continued succession of high hills with intervening valleys, so that the line is alternately carried over viaducts or through cuttings or under hills hundreds of feet in height.

North Ribblesdale, being relatively narrow and steep-sided, had just one point where the Ribble was crossed, this being north of Stainforth. The river's course was adjusted. The Settle–Carlisle line attained an elevation of 1,167 feet at Ais Gill.

The Northern Pennines are the source of an occasional blast of air known as the Helm Wind. Cooling in its progress up the Pennines, at about 15 miles per hour, it appears as a long, vaporous bar at the top of the fells, and then plunges down the 2,000-foot escarpment known as High Cup Nick to meet warmer air in Edenvale. It sometimes invaded the cabs of freight locomotives, and cobs of coal might have been blown from a fireman's shovel. Steam-hauled trains were paramount on the Settle–Carlisle in the 1950s. The majority were phased out in the early 1960s, when Dr Richard Beeching pruned our rail system—wielding what became known as the Beeching Axe.

The Settle–Carlisle is less complicated than most rail systems. Signals are nicely spaced, with plenty of room within the sections. A retired inspector told me, 'You could manage quite well, even in fog and mountain mist.' To be in the slow train from Carlisle to Settle on a summer evening was enchanting. Voices were raised as though in a litany, announcing such stations as Armathwaite, Lazonby, Little Salkeld, and Langwathby. My favourite natural sounds, in springtime, were the bubbling calls of curlews as they glided over their nesting territories.

The rainfall could be awesome and resulted in the Settle–Carlisle having a specialist 'slip and drainage' gang. In the 1920s there was a potentially dangerous slip at the southern end of Shotlock Hill tunnel; slipped clay and boulders rested on the wet clay in the cess. There had been anxiety about this possibility for some time, and the response was the installation of deep drains and the addition of a top wall. The response to a slip at Denthead in the 1930s was the building of a concrete wall.

When it snowed, the mighty Settle–Carlisle might be blocked for days on end. There was much talk about the winters of 1947, 1962, and 1963. You might see snow somewhere for nine months of the year. In 1926, a Leeds crew—after a line blockage—drove the first train to cross the top. Ais Gill signal box was completely snow-covered; at this point, the 'cross trees' of the telephone wires were the only objects sticking above the drifts. In 1931, snow lay so deep in Mallerstang that a drift attained the height of a signal. In the early 1930s, the Settle–Carlisle was issued with steel snow ploughs that fitted on the front buffer beam of a locomotive.

The high-lying districts at the heads of the dales through which the Settle–Carlisle made its way were once rich in wildlife, especially nesting wading birds. In spring, the melancholic whistle of the golden plover might be heard on the high moors, where the vegetation is thin. The whining *pee-wee* of the lapwing, known locally as tewit, announces the awakening of a new springtime. This species is usually nesting on high pastures. A housewife at the Ais Gill cottages, beside the railway, was careful when hanging out washing on the clothes line, not far from the house; she did not want to tread on a lapwing's nest and eggs.

And, of course, there were lots of sheep. A man who joined the rail service in the 1950s was still at work when all the men he had known when he was employed told of a North Ribblesdale farmer who came across one of his sheep, which was dead. He tossed it over a drystone wall that separated his land from the Settle–Carlisle line; he would claim money for compensation. It so happened that when the dead sheep became airborne, a ganger was passing on the line. He grabbed the corpse of the sheep—and tossed it back into the field!

When the Settle–Carlisle was being constructed, about 2,000 people—workers and their families—occupied a scattering of wooden huts that became grandly known as 'shanty towns'. Traces remained of those old times. At the nearby stone-and-slate Salt Lake Cottages, built by the railway company for some of its regular workers, I was shown a plain wooden desk at which workmen at Batty Green were regularly paid.

Folk tales have long fascinated me. A typical shanty hut in the Ribblehead area during the construction period was long, wooden, and with a felt 'topping' to turn the weather. Huts varied in size and format. Some had three rooms—one part being used by the hut-keeper and his family, the second part being a general community room (a place for meals, entertainment, and chatter), and the third space available for workmen who were lodgers. A central stove kept the denizens warm.

Navvies were, in the main, tough and hard-drinking types. They were not easily scared, though you might upset them by mentioning one word—smallpox. This was a disease that, if it visited a shanty town, laid low men who shortly before had gloried in their strength and good looks.

Garsdale, which would become a notable junction with the Wensleydale line, was well-patronised by cattle dealers attending sales in Scotland—mainly at Lanark, but once or twice in the Spey Valley. The cattle were delivered by rail to Garsdale station.

A lady living near Hawes drove her father, a cattle-dealer, to 't'Junction' (as the station was unofficially known). She sometimes threw a coat over her nightdress. There was companionship among dalesfolk; one chilly morning, as this woman returned from Garsdale to her Wensleydale home, an old lady living at a roadside cottage waved her down and offered her a mug of tea.

Wild weather tormented the Settle–Carlisle railway. Ted Boak (my godfather), a locomotive driver, related a tale of a gale-stricken day at the approach to Ribblehead Viaduct. He and the fireman attended to the controls and fire, and then crouched in sheltered corners of the cab to cheat the wind. For a brief time, the locomotive took care of itself.

Bishop Treacy was present on Centenary Day when a banquet took place in a marquee erected behind the station buildings at Settle. This 'Railway Bishop' recalled a journey on the footplate of a rebuilt 'Scot', the driver of which was Wee George Dransfield from Holbeck Shed. He recalled:

> Up the bank, beautifully crisp 3-cylinder beat, exhaust shooting up into the sky. Air as fresh as you only get in Ribblesdale. Sky bright blue with white fluffy clouds. Hills purple and friendly. Blea Moor tunnel, dark and damp.

O. S. Nock (known to his friends as Ozzie) recalled a crossing of Dent Head viaduct;

> I watched the old 40552 in front of us swaying and rolling as she took the curves. With screaming whistle, she led us into Rise Hill tunnel; out again on to that dizzy ledge above Garsdale to the highest water troughs in England.... The driver ... lowered his scoop at 60 mph. The tender was evidently fuller than he thought, for in seconds it had overflowed and we, on the second engine, were smothered. Involuntarily, I ducked, for the water came over in a solid cascade and hit our cab glasses with a roar rather than a splash.

Ozzie had known the Settle–Carlisle since his schooldays. In later life, he had often travelled by rail with notebook and stop-watch. In 1976, Ozzie attended a committee meeting at my home, which is within sight of the line. He surprised me by kneeling beside the broad sitting-room window, gazing fixedly across the dale to where a northbound train was moving along a slightly rising length of embankment. Presuming that my window ledge was level, he lined it up with the rail track and was re-assured that the Settle–Carlisle has, indeed, a ruling gradient of 1 in 100.

The 1950s saw the twilight of steam on the Settle–Carlisle. Freight work was relatively common, and during the holiday season normal traffic was augmented by steam-hauled Starlight Specials. A Kirkby Stephen man recalled the early 1930s and his first trip on the line. It was on a special train:

> ...a magical affair, taking folk to Leeds for a pantomime at The City Varieties. The train left Carlisle bright and early and picked up passengers from all stations to Kirkby Stephen. The pantomime they enjoyed was *Aladdin*, with Stanley Holloway as Widow Twanky.

Carlisle Citadel station has an architectural style known as 'Victorian Tudor'. The Midland was the seventh railway company to use the station. Until the amalgamation of 1923, each company organised its own traffic and maintenance facilities. British railways were nationalised in 1948. The 150th anniversary of the opening of Citadel Station occurred in 1997.

The saddest place must be St Leonard's Church in Chapel-le-Dale. Here there is a monument to the scores of men connected with the railway activity at the head of Ribblesdale; they had died during the construction period, and the churchyard was extended to accommodate them.

There were other last resting places in consecrated ground, not far from the line. At St Leonard's, the Reverend William Harper, incumbent, added his signature to many entries in the burial register. 'A gentleman of genial spirit'—he left the district in May 1871. The Reverend E. Smith was vicar when a churchyard extension was opened on land given by Lord Bective.

2

# Earliest Days: Men, Horses, and Bog-Carts

The Midland was granted a strip of land by an Act of Parliament; it was left to the company's valuers to acquire it through negotiation with the landowners. Lying to the south of Settle was the Anley estate of the Birkbecks. The head of the family was so fond of a local bridge that a railway proposal to 'blow it up' upset him. Mr Birkbeck arranged to stay on the bridge in daylight hours. Knowing that he was a Director of the Craven Bank at Settle, a message was sent to him reporting a 'run' on the Bank. He promptly set off into the town, and the bridge was demolished while he was away. Meanwhile, the first sod of the Settle–Carlisle was 'cut' at Anley.

James Farrer, who lived at Ingleborough Hall in Clapham, had an estate that extended over the hill to take in Blea Moor and Gearstones. He opposed the Settle–Carlisle Bill in 1866, but benefited greatly from the sale of land at Batty Moss—from which would spring the imposing Ribblehead Viaduct. Farrer would also draw royalties for quarried stone, for sand, and as rent for land on which hutments would be built as temporary quarters for the workers, their wives, and their children.

The men who devised and planned the route were typically Victorian in their drive and energy. James Joseph Allport, General Manager of the Midland Railway from 1860 until 1880, presided over the project. He had been lured from another railway company with the offer of a salary of £1,500 per year. He got to know the course of the line from first hand. On his retirement through ill-health, he was presented with a portrait of himself with the awesome Blea Moor in the background. Allport was retained as a consultant, and he was knighted in 1887,

John Ashwell, a contractor operating from Highgate Road in Kentish Town, successfully tendered for Contract No. 1 (Settle to Dent Head). The heaviest works—Ribblehead Viaduct and Blea Moor Tunnel—were on this stretch. The first workers were housed in the four-wheeled, horse-drawn van that came to rest at Ribblehead in December 1869. One of Ashwell's special tasks was to provide hutted accommodation for his workers, who would otherwise be unable to find accommodation in this wild area. Workers and their families in the hill country were housed in huts of great length, roofed with felt that was tarred three times a year. Some huts had porches to cheat the weather.

John Sydney Crossley, the company's engineer-in-chief who had delayed his retirement to supervise the construction work, presided over a large team. He became aware that workmen who blasted the boulder-clay like rock were, within a few hours, having 'to ladle out the same stuff from the same spot like soup in buckets'. Crossley and Allport had gone on a voyage of discovery—called prospecting—walking the greater part of the distance between Settle and Carlisle. It was found to be comparatively easy sailing until they got to Blea Moor, 'that terrible place'.

Ashwell built a Mission House. He contributed to the financial support needed by a Scripture Reader. Through his goodwill, a hospital was built and subsequently enlarged. When he got into financial trouble, the Midland company advanced him £50,000. Not being able to meet his commitments, Ashwell was released from his contract in 1871, and the generous Midland handed him £10,000. The Midland took over Contract No. 1, appointing W. H. Ashwell as agent. He was well-disposed towards labourers. In November 1869, the notable firm of Benton and Woodiwiss, securing Contract No. 2 (Dent Head to Kirkby Stephen), were considerate towards the men, establishing a coffee-room at Garsdale. Coffee, bread, and butter were distributed without charge. Also available were books, newspapers, periodicals, and games.

The course of the line had been surveyed and mapped by a small team led by Charles Stanley Sharland, a Tasmanian by birth. He was first mentioned in 1865 as a 20*s*-per-week engineer in the office of the Maryport and Carlisle Railway. Sharland led a team of surveyors from Carlisle to Settle in ten days. A delay was experienced at Gearstones, near Ribblehead; the inn where they stayed overnight was 'snowed up', and they had to dig their way out. Sharland did not live long enough to see the railway take shape. In the autumn of 1870, gravely ill with tuberculosis, he resigned; he moved to sunny Torquay and died in 1871, aged twenty-six years.

Batty Green, also known as Batty Moss, part of the Ingleborough estate, had a bleak aspect in 1869 when a four-wheeled caravan, towed from London by a steam engine, came to rest thereabouts. It was be the temporary quarters of engineers that would supervise the experimental borings for the piers of what would become the mighty Ribblehead Viaduct, and a major tunnel excavation at Blea Moor. The caravan, known grandly as the Contractor's Hotel, was a tight-fit home to ten men throughout the first winter. As darkness came, a man stationed at the caravan held up a bull's-eye lantern to guide his fellow workmen who were coming home through the waste.

In the summer of 1870, less than a year after the cutting of the first sod, the 72-mile-long strip of land between Settle and Carlisle was a confusion of men and appliances, of raw stone and deranged earth. Well over 5,000 workmen were involved, and that autumn the army of navvies had swollen to 6,255. Lots of navvies were engaged in the project, but there was a much larger and more varied workforce consisting of inspectors, clerks, cashiers, gangers, timekeepers, masons, brickmakers, carpenters, platelayers, horse-keepers, engine drivers, stokers, tippers, saddlers, mechanics, sawyers, quarrymen, cement burners, mortar grinders, and engine tenters.

A writer in *Chambers Journal* in 1873 used the Pollen family as the source of much of his information. Half past five was the hour Mrs Pollen had given him:

> I was punctual. As I came up the road from the Chum-Hole, through Inkermann to the mansion of the Pollens, the face of the swamp in the watery twilight was alive with navvies on their way home from work. They stalked carelessly through the most horrid, clinging mire.

A navvy was stated in the article to be a very rough diamond, 'but when you come to mix with him familiarly, and to understand him, you come to realise he is a diamond'. An engineer who claimed to know him 'to his very marrow' added that the English navvy had his bad points:

> Very bad points, they are, no doubt, but as a rule they all have a common origin. The fountain of all, or almost all, the troubles of an English employer of this description of labour is the ale-can.

This writer also mentioned lassies who climbed Ingleborough and then sat round a huge coal fire in Mrs Pollen's keeping-room:

> It was a state occasion; and the six navvies, who are lodgers, were relegated to their own sleeping apartment where I found Mr Pollen, slightly fresher from his journey to Ingleton, having his hair cut by one of the lodgers prior to entering the sphere of gentility in the other room.

The main part of this story was of the intervention of a drunken navvy. He was eventually thrown out.

Two of the shanty towns set up in a wild part of Blea Moor were named Sebastopol and Inkerman, implying that some of the residents had been involved in wartime work in the Crimea. Most families living in the shanties were pretty rough—unkempt and unwashed. Hens scattered about some of the huts. Mice and rats were not uncommon denizens of the rafters. A correspondent of the *Lancaster Guardian* noted that the numerous huts that dotted the moor were known as Batty Green, Sebastopol, Jericho, Jerusalem, and Tunnel Huts. The name of one of the huts had a Mormon tinge, being known as Salt Lake —an area in the New World where a host of Mormons had set up homes. Not far from Batty Green is a group of stone and slate railway houses known as Salt Lake Cottages.

At Batty Green stood the contractor's offices, yard, stables, store rooms, and shops. Also existing hereabouts, in due course, were places of social importance—a mission room, day and Sunday schools, a public library, a post office, shops, and the aforementioned hospital—which was new and neat-looking, with a covered walk for convalescent patients. The mortuary was provided with coffins. A visitor found someone lying in a coffin; he touched the 'corpse', who replied, 'Can't you leave a person alone?' The man, dead drunk, had climbed into the coffin for a nap.

In 1870, James Tiplady, a missionary, arrived at Batty Green, being paid a modest £100 per year plus a free pass from Settle to Bradford—and back—once a month. Initially, he emulated John Wesley and preached in the open air, operating in a strip of railway country with a length of 17 miles. Tiplady was provided with a room for services, and he organised Penny Readings on Saturday evenings. Some people would sing, others would recite, and a third group indulged in telling jokes. A night school was organised, and Sunday and day schools were opened. William Fletcher, another Scripture reader, was based at Kirkby Stephen. The two men had been selected from a list of over 200 applicants.

Dr James Riley, born and reared at Settle, recalled that in his childhood he had overheard many first-class accounts of the building of the line and the camps of the navvies. A member of the Walton family, who was known as Tommy Shop Charlie, set off with a van-load of bread for the hutted camp on Batty Moss. Also related was an account of the first locomotive being dragged along Chapel-le-Dale from Ingleton by a team of twenty horses. In 1873, Contract No. 1 (Settle Junction to Denthead) had about 2,300 workers—and no less than 130 horses.

The aforementioned bog-cart, based on an idea that pre-dated railways, was described by historian F. S. Williams as 'a huge barrel over which was a light cart-body and shafts, so arranged that as the horse pulled it, the barrel would turn like a gigantic garden roller'. Usually filled 'with victuals, or clothes, or bricks,' this device was able to negotiate soggy ground 'where no wheels could go'. Williams had often seen 'three horses in a row pulling at that concern over the moss till they sank up to their middle and had to be drawn out, one at a time, by their necks, to save their lives'.

Contract No. 2 extended from Dent Head to Kirkby Stephen, taking in Mallerstang, where the first sod was cut by the agent of Lord Hothfield of Appleby. Water that gushed off Wild Boar Fell descended by what became known as the Golden Culvert. 'It cost a lot of money to make—and it wasn't cheap to maintain'. Artengill Viaduct spanned a deep and rugged gill. Contract No. 3 (Smardale to Crowdundle) took in a tunnel at Crosby Garrett that had to be driven through solid rock, a mixture of limestone and grit. Contract No. 4 (Crowdundle to Durranhill) involved the Barren Park Cutting, which was through red sandstone, was 42 feet at its deepest place, and nearly a mile in length.

Justice was meted out severely to any railway labourers brought before a magisterial bench, composed of stern landowners and notable businessmen. At Appleby, the redoubtable W. Crackenthorpe, whose estate was involved in the route of the new railway, sentenced a navvy to a week's hard labour; the man had been charged with sleeping on a hayrick. Some of the local navvies had wild ways. In October 1872, a navvy called Charles Fox, in custody at Kirkby Stephen, was charged with the theft of a valuable terrier. The prisoner was traced by the police to Denthead, where he had sold the dog for beer. He claimed the animal had followed him.

3

# Track-laying: Permanent Way

An engineer compared the Settle–Carlisle railway with a whale lying on its belly; its nose was at Settle and the tail was at Carlisle. The railway extended from Settle Junction to Petteril Bridge, a distance of rather more than 72 miles. About two-thirds of the line lay in the county of Cumbria. The ruling gradient on the Drag from Settle to Ais Gill was fixed at 1 in 100. The first sod was, as mentioned, cut near Anley. The date was in November 1869. The first sod to be lifted in Westmorland was on the property of Sir Richard Tufton, of Appleby Castle. The area was Mallerstang, and the spade in use was wielded by Mr Parkin Blades, who was the estate agent.

Railway work raised the echoes in the region. An embankment extending from near Settle church towards Langcliffe absorbed 1,000,000 cubic yards of earth. The level of the rail at the summit was 1,167 feet above sea level. Beyond Armathwaite, in the far north, lay an embankment containing nearly 400,000 cubic yards of material. Messrs Benton and Woodiwiss, the contractors twixt Dent Head and Kirkby Stephen, used a locomotive they had received by rail at Sedbergh in 1873 for earth work. The loco, named *Larne*, had been hauled to Garsdale Head by a score of horses.

The rail-track, known as 'Permanent Way', was laid in 60-yard lengths, being bedded down in 1875 by a train of the 'goods' variety. Many of the plain rails came from the steel works at Workington. Points and crossings were made by Taylor Brothers, of Sandiacre, near Nottingham. The spikes became troublesome, working loose; wooden plugs tended to split and break. Sleepers were creosoted under pressure in large metal cylinders.

Fifty to sixty men gathered for a large re-laying job when a rail 60 feet long was to be used. Permanent way inspectors were active, looking for men who might be idle. A typical, old-time platelayer wore a coarse shirt and fustian trousers—tied beneath the knees by 'yorks'. These allowed freedom of movement for knees and legs, whilst ensuring the trouser legs did not drag in the mud. The platelayer was shod with heavy, hob-nailed boots.

A regular passenger service began in the May of 1876; church bells at Appleby rang out in celebration. Aptly-named lengthmen—four or five in a gang—kept a daily eye on appointed sections of the track, attending to any damage that occurred. Rails near signals were changed regularly—in some cases every few months. A lengthman remarked, 'Once a locomotive's wheels started to spin, you couldn't stop them. I've seen metal that was white hot with friction.' It was considered a blessing to come across an area where a level line could be constructed for nearly half a mile. An example was stretch between Helwith Bridge and Horton.

Many skilled men worked on the viaducts that were rooted deep in soft ground until bedrock was reached. Joiners provided the wooden scaffolding that enabled men to work at various heights. Deaths were soon being reported. In the graveyard at Settle Church, with lettering that has since become indistinct, is a stone marking the grave of John Griffith Owen, a Welshman who died at the age of nineteen. He had been hit by the massive arm of a crane as a party of men worked in the deep cutting at Langcliffe.

A mason used hammer and trowel. Stone blocks, some weighing over 5 tons, were delivered to him by a steam-operated 'traveller', which, on a viaduct, might smoothly lift a huge stone for 70 feet or more. Vertical steam engines, assembled at the head of tunnel shafts on Blea Moor or Rise Hill, were used at the surface to haul up material excavated from the headings. Locomotives, with rakes of trucks, chugged across tramways. Some of the horses were set to work hauling spoil from the tunnels.

Some good stone was found 'on the doorstep', but, later, a goodly amount of granite was imported from North Wales. Many plain rails were imported, as mentioned, from the steel works at Workington. Points and 'crossings' were made by Taylor Brothers at Sandiacre, near Nottingham. There was a period when Douglas fir and Baltic pine were being imported to provide sleepers. Consigned to a large depot at Beeston, near Nottingham, a sleeper was taken to a machine that bored six holes simultaneously. Sleepers were then creosoted under pressure in large metal cylinders.

New sleepers were placed at the trackside. Men working on piece-rates, recruited in advance and using a gauge, attached iron 'chairs' to the sleepers. They bored holes with an auger, put on the chairs, and placed a spike in one hole and a plug in the other. 'Nippers' were employed to tar the plugs and spikes, and put them ready 'for the men to knock in'.

Night accommodation was needed for a host of workers. Before the First World War, a man might lodge out in summer at a charge of 1 *s* per night. There were breaks for meals during a working day. Harry Cox of Settle recalled to me that, as a young man, he was away from home for days on end. His mother filled a small box with food. When he opened the box, he saw, at a glance, the meals that would be available, day by day, in the following week.

Platelayers between Skipton and Hawes replaced the old railroad with a new road. A gang knocked out the chocks. Several men followed, tipping rail out of the chocks. Another gang picked up a rail and carried it to the side of the track. The old sleepers were removed by yet another gang. New track was now in use, fish plates being fitted to join the rails. In the 1930s, a platelayer received 40 *s* a week, 'less 1 *s* 1 *d* insurance, 9 *d* health and 4 *d* unemployment'. In 1937, when a gang of sixty men undertook a re-laying job on the branch line from Garsdale to Hawes, temporary men were paid two guineas per week. When they were made 'permanent' shortly afterwards, the wage for an individual was reduced to £2 per week.

A regular Settle–Carlisle gang usually consisted of a ganger and four men, though at a large station like Hellifield or Skipton there would be six men with a ganger in charge. A typical workman wore corduroy trousers, tied below the knee, a union shirt with a neckerchief or muffler, a well-used jacket, and a hat, usually of the Billycock type. Subsequently, when the railway was operational, platelayers were allocated to the various lengths, each length providing men with the facility of a cabin. There was a popular chant: 'During fog or falling snow, into the cabin you must go'.

A cabin was situated beside each length of rail and close to each large viaduct or tunnel. Each cabin had one door, one window, and one chimney. Under cover, the ganger picked the best seat. He was not always present. He had to 'look the length' each morning; if it was raining, he'd get wet through, and the workers would remain nice and dry. Dick Fawcett told me that some cabins were stone-built. Dent was one of them, the stone cabins being built with men engaged on snow-clearing work in mind.

Other huts were made of sleeper-wood, the roof being covered by thick felt or occasionally with slates. A writer in 1870 noted described wooden huts as they were at Ribblehead:

> Wooden huts and stabling have been erected, tommy shops are opening, wagons laden with material are constantly passing to and fro and the shouts of the teamsters and the stroke of the pick are becoming familiar to the ears.

A remotely situated cabin was snugly-sited in the navvy-made ravine just short of Blea Moor Tunnel. This cabin had white-washed interior walls. Down at Skipton were some 'old salt cabins' in which drivers might stay for an hour or so in the dead of night, while waiting to 'relieve' a train from Carlisle. Sometimes, a railman heard rats running about. When one chap lay down to sleep, a rat ran across his legs. As rain fell, the men smoked or played cards. A popular game was called 'nap'.

The Midland Railway type of iron stove, which was square-shaped, might be found fitted to the interiors of signal boxes. Such a stove—which was square, with a little flap in front—provided the workers with warmth and heated their lunchtime food. A kettle was placed on top and there'd be a pie or two in the attendant oven. Platelayers sat around the stove, and periodically spat into the fire. A foreman had usually allowed a man to go to the local cabin an hour before bait (meal) time to prepare food for the men. Each man was asked what he was having. One reply was: 'Half a collop of bacon and a couple of eggs, plus some bread we got from our lodgings.'

Men who were temporarily off-duty would sit around a stove, occasionally spitting into the flames. Some smoked black twist, a form of tobacco, which meant that the atmosphere was 'pretty thick'. Some slept—and snored. Other men would be carding, gambling for pennies. The ordinary navvy's fare was bread and cheese or beef sandwiches. A well-known hut, at the lineside in Mallerstang, was known as Hangman's Cabin; a depressed man had hanged himself.

The permanent way men living beside the Settle–Carlisle were adept at attracting the attention of footplate crews on passing locomotives when coal was required for the cabin fire. During a prolonged, frosty spell, Simon Fothergill, who, with others, cautioned footplate men not to travel fast, contracted pneumonia and died. His widow augmented her small income by taking in lodgers. Dick Fawcett fared rather better than that—he told me, 'I'd put a kettle on the stove or a pie in the oven.'

An old-time railwayman who was recalled by Dick had frequently taken off his belt to beat his wife. He set off to his track-work one morning without the belt—it had been nowhere to be seen. What had happened to it was evident at lunchtime; his pie—and some others—had been heated in the stove by the ganger, who had arrived at the hut ahead of the men. The pie of the wife-beater was emitting a strong smell. She had surreptitiously slipped fragments of the missing belt into the pie!

Ted Boak of Skipton, who drove powerful locomotives, mentioned that the fireman who accompanied him on the footplate had the task of breaking up especially large pieces of coal. Feeding lumps of coal to platelayers' huts was not uncommon. There was a ganger in Mallerstang who said to Ted, 'Will you throw me off a bit o' coal off?'

Ted said, 'Aye. Where do you want it?'

'In the middle cabin', he replied.

The next morning, Ted had three or four great big cobs o' coal standing up. 'Just before we got to that cabin, off they went—right through the doorway!'

Old Adam, the ganger on one branch, kept an eye open for the permanent way inspector —a sly man, who was 'always creeping about, trying to catch men who were doing nothing'. His tendency to skulk in ditches led to the nickname Mickey Mouse. Adam said, 'One way of stopping him entering a cabin was to heat up t'sneck so it would be too hot to handle'.

Sparks from locomotives, falling on tinder-dry vegetation along the embankments, caused many a fire, putting signalling equipment and fences at risk. Local tradesmen, who relied on horses to draw their carts and who could not afford to buy land on which to make hay as fodder, took leases on sections of the embankments. With such leases, the Midland was able to keep its embankments tidy and reduce the risk of fire. Bill Jackman, of Langcliffe, used an old-fashioned, straight-shafted scythe. As the mown grass dried, it tumbled down the embankment.

When the Second World War began, the line was in good condition; much of it had been re-laid. The first long-welded track was laid just south of Settle in 1956. A piece then went into the line at Selside. The railtracks have shivered with the passage of coal trains operating between Scotland and power stations in England. There were 'gypsum' trains from power stations heading for a processing industry at Kirkby Thore. Specialist gangs of men maintained the railway. The so-called Slip and Drainage Gang did their best to cope with the awesome Pennine rainfall.

4

# Viaducts and Tunnels: Rails Go Underground

Midland Railway's triumphs of engineering consisted of twenty viaducts, fourteen tunnels, and no sharp bends.

## Ribblehead Viaduct

Batty Green, a tract of land lying where Ribblesdale meets up with Chapel-le-Dale, became a major centre of railway activity. The first sign of activity was when a van—known as the Contractor's Hotel—appeared beside Batty Moss. It was a lodging place for men who would survey the land and, especially, a focal point for work on Ribblehead Viaduct. What had been a habitat for sheep and grouse would become a large industrial site. A mini-railway system would connect the dale road, the massive viaduct, and a major tunnel that would put a hole through Blea Moor.

The viaduct arches would be lined with red bricks. Some were made locally, but later darker and more durable bricks from Lancashire would be introduced. The viaduct construction was managed by Charles and Walter Hurst, who had a workforce of 100 at any given time, including sixty skilled Welshmen. In March 1872 they went on strike for a short time, demanding better wages.

The viaduct, 'Bridge 66', would be popularly known as Ribblehead Viaduct. It was well-designed, with every sixth pier thicker than the others. If one pier collapsed it would, theoretically, take only five other piers with it. The viaduct, built from north to south, was completed in 1875—an event marked by the setting of a large stone bearing that date at the centre of the parapet. Steep embankments on each end of the viaduct were sown with a ryegrass mix.

A train named *Diamond,* the first intended for passengers, ran across the new viaduct during an experimental trip in April 1876. On board were the driver, a stoker, a guard, and five passengers. One of the green-painted locomotives designed by Matthew Kirtley earned distinction by hauling a Pullman drawing room and sleeping cars from Skipton to Carlisle in two hours and five minutes. The average speed was 43 miles per hour. Alas, Matthew Kirtley did not live to see his creation storm The Long Drag. He died at his office in 1873.

The viaduct would originally be named after Batty Moss. A twenty-four arched viaduct—1,328 feet long and around 100 feet high—stood firm against strong westerly gales. The main Ingleton-Hawes road would pass under Archway No. 13. Viaduct and Blea Moor Tunnel were in an area for which negotiations had taken place between James Allport, the Midland Railway Company's general manager, and James Farrer, of Ingleborough Estate. Allport was not a squeamish man; he became known as the Bismark of Railway Politics. Visiting the hills that would be crossed by the railway, he remarked:

> I shall never forget, as long as I live, the difficulties surrounding the undertaking ... We walked over the greatest part of the line from Settle to Carlisle and found it comparatively easy sailing—till we got to that terrible place, Blea Moor.

So great was the planned Ribblehead viaduct that work began immediately after the contract had been signed. Seventy trial borings were made during the winter of 1869–70. Shafts were sunk through peat and clay to solid rock, a few being fixed on concrete. Building the viaduct took place from north to south. The piers which emerged from the shafts were enmeshed in a timber frame to facilitate building, and also to enable the builders to use a 'steam traveller' to lift the blocks of limestone to their appointed places.

Blocks of dark limestone had been dug from a quarry in Little Dale Beck. The arches that were formed were given brick underlays, although bricks made locally were found to be unsatisfactory, and those that were exposed to weathering were fitted with a darker variety—known as Accrington reds. It was estimated that, when finished, the structure would consist of 30,000 cubic yards of masonry and 3,000 cubic yards of concrete.

When I met Harry Cox in January 1976, he related some of his vivid memories of the start of a working life between 1905 and 1910:

> I helped to re-brick the most northerly arches of Ribblehead Viaduct. It was a time when we had to lodge out in summer and were paid 1 shilling a night to cover the cost.

Workmen faced strong winds from the west. Harry said:

> These winds came racing up Chapel-le-Dale. The arches seem to suck them through. Work on the viaduct had to stop and every small item—tools, etc.—were removed or secured firmly.

When the work was done, a goods train passed:

> A door on a van must not have been properly closed for it blew open. Lots of boxes with kippers came flying out. We should have collected the boxes and taken them to the station. Some of them were delivered. We also managed to live off kippers for weeks!

Almost as imposing as the stonework were the embankments on either side.

During the construction period, workers had filled in with earth a pothole known as Batty Wife Hole, which had been in effect a pond. A local legend was born. A Mrs Batty, a farmer's wife, had done her washing here. She and her husband were always arguing and eventually she 'walked out'; he pleaded with her to return. They decided to meet again at the side of the pothole. When he did not appear, she became terribly upset, leapt into the pool, and was drowned. Along came the husband, who had been held up by another job. When he was told what had happened, he too jumped in the pool—and was taken out dead.

During a time of conservation, when brickwork was being attended to and worn stones were being replaced, I was given permission, in the company of Peter Fox, an old friend, to ascend fixed ladders and walk on scaffolding. The weather had calmed down. The workmen came from Lancashire. I marvelled at their skill and at the workmanship that had gone into the best-known of the Settle–Carlisle viaducts.

A man who was attending to Accrington bricks pointed to a gap created by two that were especially worn. I was told that blue tits nested there. A ledge running along the topside of the viaduct had been cleaned; it must have been used as a resting or roosting place for birds, because it had held living strawberries. I saw a piece of limestone that reminded me of the viaduct's ancient origins. On the limestone was a pattern of shellfish that had lived hereabouts at a time when everything was still under water.

Jack Towler, who spent his boyhood on a farm between Ingleton and Bentham, went to work on the Settle–Carlisle in the summer of 1924. By then, his family had left the farm; they were living at Stone House, between Selside and Salt Lake Cottages. Jack walked to work. His first day had been spent on Ribblehead Viaduct. George Cockerill, a ganger, had come to Ribblehead from Newmarket and was given charge of a team of five platelayers. They used muscles rather than machines to move rails and sleepers: 'We'd gangs o' men to pick rails up for loading on to wagons. They then had to pick t'chaired sleepers up. Six men to a sleeper ... Today it's all done by machinery.' George felt Ribblehead Viaduct trembling in certain places when trains were passing: 'Frost used to lift the lines a bit, especially at the southern end.'

Jack Towler and his wife returned from their honeymoon in 1932. They had been allowed accommodation at Salt Lake. Fog swirled around the head of the dale. Jack was called out in the middle of the night for fogging duties, and in 1939 he became a ganger. There was no electricity at home. After dark, the living room held the glow of a paraffin lamp. The Salt Lakers, like so many in those days, bathed in zinc baths that were set before roaring fires. The Dawson children, who had a railwayman father, lived at a railway cottage near Blea Moor tunnel; they had to pass under a viaduct arch daily on their way to school. At times, they felt like waiting a while, hoping the funnelled wind would abate. They even had the ruse of slipping lumps of stone into the pockets of their coats to weigh them down.

Signalmen heading for Blea Moor box had the same trouble with howling gales. 'Gale men', who gathered south of Blea Moor to await the arrival of a 'down' goods train, had the train directed into a loop. The wagon sheets must be checked—as a train crossed the viaduct in windy weather, a wagon sheet might be ripped or torn away, floating across the fells like an autumn leaf, a windfall in a literal sense to any local farmer who was around when they came to earth. A railway maintenance man recalled when planks on the scaffolding, erected for repair work, and affected by the wind, 'went up and down like piano keys'.

## Dent Head

The viaduct, at Dent Head, north of Blea Moor, has ten spans, a length of 596 feet, and a maximum height of 100 feet. A blue variety of limestone, quarried locally, was used for the masonry. The viaduct is crossed by trains that have burst out of—or, heading south, are about to enter—Blea Moor Tunnel. No one really notices the fine viaduct—they are usually enraptured by the broad view of a glorious dalehead. Motorists are also awestruck because the road passes through one of the viaduct arches. A fascinating feature at the base of the viaduct is a single-span bridge, an arch formed of slabs of stone. It was not given a parapet, for in the old days it would have been crossed by packhorse teams—which, incidentally, were also occasionally known as trains!

## Arten Gill

Arten Gill viaduct, also at the side of the valley of the Dee, spans a deep and rugged gill. The viaduct has a length of 660 feet, eleven spans, and a maximum height of 117 feet. An Act of Parliament in 1871 granted a deviation; the structure would otherwise have had a height of 167 feet. This imposing viaduct is formed of a dark limestone known as Dent Marble, which, when polished, shows up fossils in white relief. Difficulty was encountered in getting firm foundations for the piers—some were set over 55 feet below the surface of the ground. In the construction period, immense blocks of limestone, excavated in a quarry at the bottom of the gill, were conveyed by bogies to the staging and put in place on the emerging viaduct by a steam traveller.

Arten Gill was inclined to lift in frosty weather. Flagmen kept the speed of trains that were passing over the viaduct to 15 miles per hour. One driver had been heard comparing the sensation of driving across it in frosty weather with passing over a corrugated roof. In 1835, William George Armstrong and his wife, Margaret, on their honeymoon from Newcastle, ventured into the Gill. Angling was his favourite sport. The machinery being used at Arten Gill to recover stone impressed this young man, who would become the founder of the huge Armstrong engineering works in the North East.

## Dandry Mire

An embankment was proposed for the well-named Dandry Mire, to the north of Garsdale station. Mire is a term for mossland. Tipping went on for over two years. Instead of a solid embankment being formed, the peaty nature of the area received over 250,000 cubic yards of tipped material. It became necessary to construct a viaduct in the deepest part of the Moss. Six arches were created; each had a span of 45 feet, the greatest depth being 53 feet.

## Smardale Viaduct

Draping itself over the valley of the Scandal Beck, in a dozen grand arches, is Smardale Viaduct. The height of the viaduct is 130 feet—35 feet less than the celebrated Ribblehead viaduct. Great viaducts were constructed using heavy timber staging. An unexpected difficulty arose when the Smardale viaduct was being constructed; John Crossley noted that the river had appeared to be running over solid rock. Instead of rock, the builders had to go down through 45 feet of clay until they came to the red shale, 'and upon it we built'.

The last stone of Smardale viaduct was laid by Agnes Crossley in June 1875. Details of the deed were carved on the stone—along with the date, which was 8 June 1875. In its construction, over a spell of five years, the viaduct had absorbed 60,000 tons of limestone, taken from a quarry about a mile upstream. Some of the trial boreholes probed for 20 feet to the underlying rock.

## Moorcock

A viaduct first named Dandry Mire, which cuts across the head of Garsdale with considerable visual impact, was given the name Moorcock—a local name for red grouse, the hostelry being at the junction between the Hawes-Sedbergh highway and the one that heads northwards, via Mallerstang, to Kirkby Stephen. Kit Calvert, the sage of upper Wensleydale, had heard that towards the end of the eighteenth century, and in the early part of the nineteenth, this was one of two public houses that sheltered Scottish drovers as they travelled southwards with cattle and sheep. A tragic railway incident occurred in December 1910; the Scots express was wrecked, and ten disfigured bodies were carried into the Moorcock. The inn was once a meeting place of the Lunesdale Foxhounds. In the 1970s the inn was gutted by fire, but it then rose, phoenix-like, from the ashes, to remain a popular meeting place.

## Lunds

In the old Midland days, scaffolding used on Lunds viaduct was moved on bogeys to Garsdale, thence down the Hawes branch. A flagman stationed down the line cautioned trains about this special traffic. The driver of one goods train failed to see the flagman; men with the bogeys were suddenly aware that a train was approaching, being no more than half a mile away. They managed to jump to one side before, being fiercely braked, the train collided with the bogeys. Scaffolding was spread across the track. The driver of the goods train was suspended from work.

## Eden Lacy Viaduct

Eden Lacy Viaduct occupies a glorious situation. About a quarter of a mile away, a three-arched ornamental bridge spanned the line as an occupational way for Col. Sanderson, of Eden Lacy House. It enabled him to pass with ease from one part of his park to the other. The bridge was constructed of red sandstone, the piers and arches being faced with rustic quoins.

Bridges with wooden staging were erected in Mallerstang.

> T'local ganger was capped when farmers were always getting sheep killed there. He was particular about fences. Nowt much else could get through 'em. He waited yance ower. He'd seen a dead sheep somewhere. Then he saw a farmer coming over t'bridge wi' t'sheep. He lifted a loose board on bridge and dropped t'dead sheep through on to the line. They'd do owt for a bit o' brass.

## Taitlands

And so to tunnels… Some of the finest engineering work was lost to sight as trains rattled through a confined space in the holes driven through the hills. One of the shortest tunnels is Taitlands, at Stainforth, the tunnel's length being 120 yards, taking in a crossing of the North Craven Fault. The tunnel also extends beneath the grounds of a large house that became a youth hostel and returned to private ownership. Some visitors had a feeling that a ghost was near when they heard rumbling sounds while walking on the lawn between the house and the dale road. It was explained to them that the sound came from a passing train that was still climbing on this stretch of the Long Drag. In the 1880s, when the tunnel was being excavated, the Midland provided the family who lived in the large house with the cost of a holiday. At Taitlands, northward-bound trains emerge from the tunnel into a deep, rock cutting.

## Blea Moor

The best-known tunnel on the Settle–Carlisle must be Blea Moor. I once had the joy of walking through it with an inspector and regular inspection party. The up-line was closed to rail traffic; a steam-hauled goods train thundered by on the other track. The engineer in charge of our inspection party suggested that I might tuck the lower end of my trousers into my stockings to avoid smoke entering and pouring out from under my clothes.

Later, an old-time railwayman who knew the tunnel said:

> Blea Moor? It's the weirdest place you could be in when the 'steamers' were running. The place stunk o' sulphur. There was a sound of dripping

> water—or dead silence. One of the tunnel men would say: 'A train's coming—south end, lads.' Then, after a bit: 'Train coming north end.' After that it was so gloomy we could hardly stir. We'd all sorts of jobs to do in Blea Moor. None of 'em was of the type to make you smile.

Blea Moor is a rounded hill north of Ribblehead Viaduct. With Victorian verve and precious little equipment beyond sticks of dynamite, shovels, and the muscles of men, a tunnel with a length of 2,629 yards was driven through the moor, reaching a point 500 feet below the moor-top. The tunnel was hewn out with Victorian verve by about 300 miners, bricklayers, and labourers. They cut through gritstone, shale, and limestone. A thin vein of coal was found.

Tunnel men were at work from each end of Blea Moor between 1870 and 1875. The work was continuous from Sunday night until Saturday night, and the tunnelling process cost £45 per yard. Ramblers see evidence of it when they are walking over the moor. The tunnel's maximum depth below the moor-top is 500 feet. Into view, protruding above each of three air shafts, are red-brick extensions, covered with iron netting.

When I joined the inspection party, viewing the shafts from below, I saw these shafts— 10 feet in diameter—had been fitted with garlands to catch water and lead it into fall-pipes, from which it would flow into the main drains. In the construction period, three shafts had provided the workers with six headings. The steam engines fixed at the top of each shaft were of the type used when making city sewers. At Blea Moor they were also available to draw trucks containing coal up the fellside.

It had been a dismally foggy day when I joined the tunnel group at Blea Moor. We quit the fog that clung to the moors for tunnel smoke. Standing on the 'up' line, which was closed to traffic, was a cattle wagon modified as a platform, from which men tested the masonry with spear-like ends to long rods, fashioned from worn-out shovels. An attached wagon held wedges, cement, and bricks. A seated inspector with writing materials recorded any needy jobs. The tunnel had a crown, haunches, and sidewalls. Tablets on the sidewalls noted the distance from the tunnel mouth at the southern end. Any part of the masonry might have its location noted precisely.

From high above the tracks came the chanting of men who were reporting on the state of the masonry. 'Hold it, lads,' came a muffled shout—and some soft masonry was brought down, while the position was noted so it might be repaired. The man-powered wagons rumbled through a gloom that was relieved by paraffin lamps. At the bottom of shaft No. 3, which is 10 feet in diameter, I had the novelty of looking upwards for 390 feet, the distance from rail to moor. This shaft, and two others I would see eventually, was marked at intervals with 'garlands' that intercepted rainwater and led it into a fall-pipe, connecting it with the main drains of the tunnel.

During my conducted walk through Blea Moor Tunnel, I heard three blasts on a whistle. 'Train on the down!' someone yelled. I felt compression on my ear-drums. There was a shriek from the locomotive, a sound that reverberated through the huge cavern. Someone shouted, 'Clear the six foot!' There was a danger that the sheet on one of the passing wagons would be flapping, hurtful if a man was struck and the train was moving at 50 or 60 miles per hour.

I heard another train whistle. This time it was much nearer. A giant locomotive thundered past, only a few yards from where we stood. Firelight stained the darkness. There was a staccato clattering of wagons. Then, silence—a silence intensified by smoke that swept down from the head of the tunnel, blotting out the friendly circle of light on one of the ventilation shafts. The moaning monster seemed to fill half the tunnel to within a few inches of the roof. It was travelling fast enough to draw most of the smoke behind it.

I had been advised to tuck the lower part of my trousers into my stockings ('or you'll have smoke pouring from underneath your collar'). That day I saw the remains of a gong that had been installed as a warning device when an outer distant signal was placed in the tunnel early in the Second World War—a warning to footplate men to look for this signal. 'The gong never worked properly. Eventually, a signal was put inside the tunnel.'

Blea Moor came into the mind of a member of the Preston family and myself when, long years ago, we had discussed the railway, and I heard that my companion's grandfather had been a nipper (a young lad who ran errands). This nipper entered the upper reaches of Blea Moor at a time when tunnel work was in hand. He would leave one of the shanty camps at Ribblehead and ascend by tramway to where men were lowering and lifting objects using a large vertical engine at the head of the shaft. The engine was 'like a boiler with a chimney above it'. It was fed by coal and provided steam, which in turn gave power to the ups and downs of the shaft. This nipper went down the shaft in a large basket, meeting the miners who were using the new type of explosive called dynamite to blast their way.

Tunnelling was a meticulous job, costing an estimated £45 per yard. In driving the tunnel, miners reached a point 500 feet below the top of the moor, working by candlelight. The bill for candles averaged £50 per month. Holes for the explosives were drilled by hand. Dynamite, then a novelty, bought for £200 per ton, was packed into the holes and ignited by means of a time fuse. A major part of the dynamite cost was for transportation from Newcastle to Carlisle. The excavators came across veins of lead, and also a small vein of coal. One of the carters working at the north end of the tunnel had suffered badly when the wheels of the cart went over a leg, which was badly severed. His friends picked him up, transporting him from the scene on a small cart drawn by a horse. They conveyed him around the fell to a shanty town. 'There was blood dripping off the cart all the way. The poor man died.'

When two ends of the tunnel were joined, there was a difference of around 3 inches—and the underground temperature fell by 23 degrees. The surveyors were fearful of breaking into an uncharted underground spring. There was precious little equipment beyond shovels and sticks of dynamite, which were said to look like potted lobster. Some of the side walls were bricked; elsewhere, the arches were turned in solid rock. During the excavation period, a workman had lost his life when a sudden violent thunderstorm filled the northern heading. When his body was located, his mouth was found to be stopped up with clay.

During the steam age, about 100 trains per day passed through Blea Moor Tunnel, adding layers of soot and clogging the air with acrid smoke. I was told, 'Blea Moor was the weirdest place you could be in when the 'steamers' were running. The place stunk o' sulphur.' These words were uttered by one of the tunnel men, who added, 'You could tell a train was entering t'tunnel by the compression on your eardrums.' Before reaching the tunnel, the loco fire was built up. The fireman did not want to replenish it as the locomotive ran through 2,629 feet of darkness. 'If the wind was the wrong way—for you —and the loco was slipping a lot, all the exhaust gases came back into the cab with a choking effect for the crew.'

The smoke might hang about for days. Tunnel workmen, in the old steam days, found that smoke from passing trains—especially double-headed trains—could reduce visibility to zero. A member of the Tunnel Gang was paid half a crown per week extra and provided with thigh-length leggings for working in Blea Moor.

Sulphur was a substance that damaged the rails, leading to their replacement every four years. Tunnel air was usually damp, and the wheels of a train got to skidding. At one time, the rails were taken out and their weight was checked. I was told, 'If they got down to a certain weight they must be replaced. Rails lose condition fast in a tunnel.' Water, seeping into the north end of the tunnel, created impressive icicles. Some of them had a width of 18 inches. One of the winter tasks of the length-gang was, in a particularly cold spell, to knock any icicles down, using long poles. It was a dangerous job, for a large icicle might descend in big lumps.

The first time one of the footplate men drove an engine in the tunnel, he was rolled to the side of the cab and 'smashed [his] false teeth; that's how bad it was!' Harry Cox, labouring in Blea Moor tunnel prior to 1914, told me that naphtha lamps were used:

> ...if a man felt a little devilish he would accidentally knock one over, causing a spectacular blaze. If he felt even more devilish, he would throw something out of the darkness and knock over one or two lamps. Then the tunnel seemed to be on fire! Some men spurned the lamps. They were accustomed to walking through the tunnel in darkness, using the four-foot, tapping a rail with a stick to maintain the right course.

When an express was passing through the tunnel it was almost certain that one of the catering staff would hurl out unwanted food. 'We heard it swish against the tunnel wall. It was against regulations, of course.' One day men went into Blea Moor Tunnel with their naphtha lamps and saw something glistening ahead; it turned out to be an enormous catfish. 'We carried it back to the cabin. It was hung up there for a day or two but we didn't sample it. We wondered why the cook on that train had thrown it away in the first place.'

Jack Dawson was a member of the Tunnel Gang who, in winter, did not see daylight during the working day. He would enter the tunnel in the early morning, when it was dark, and he'd come out in the late afternoon, when it was also dark. Jack got 9 *s* a week extra on his wage; this was known to the men as 'muck money'. When it was too grim for work, maintenance men would cower in a cave-like area known as the Donkey Hole. The men readily adapted themselves to a gloomy world. Not much light came down the ventilation shafts, and the first 400 yards of the tunnel curved. Anyone working from that end would soon lose the blob of daylight.

Bill Davison, an old friend who was living in retirement at Langcliffe, was for thirteen years a member of the tunnel maintenance gang, which consisted of five men. The Davisons moved to Blea Moor from Garsdale in 1933, their home being one of the Blea Moor cottages, situated more than a mile from Ribblehead. Towards the end of the 1930s, Bill and his fellow workers were supplied with white flannel overcoats in addition to bib and brace overalls. In the days of Bill's railway life, the tunnel men carried tin duck lamps. They created a tremendous amount of smoke, but were preferable to the naphtha lamps they succeeded, which tended to burst into flames. There was always the problem from passing trains—thick, cloying, colourless smoke that took its time to clear from the tunnel. It was especially dense when double-headed trains were passing. In thick smoke, a man would progress by tapping a stick on the edge of a rail.

Letters for Blea Moor railway homes were delivered by the Chapel-le-Dale postman, operating on foot. The family shopping was undertaken in

Settle, groceries being ordered and delivered to Ribblehead station once a month. From here they were transported to Blea Moor by a freight train, which stopped at all points on the line. Mrs Davison recalled when she had to walk along the lineside from Blea Moor to Ribblehead station. More than once she had crossed the huge viaduct with a baby in her arms. Bill Davison, who was a Methodist local preacher, often carried his bicycle across the viaduct. When he planned to preach at Dent, he would carry it through Blea Moor tunnel. He knew the times of the trains, and there was not much traffic on a Sunday.

Harry Cox had mentioned that now and again a locomotive driver would report water pouring down a ventilation shaft; 'This meant that some of the garlands had been blocked. We had to de-block them.' The men went to the top of the shaft on Blea Moor, erected some scaffolding, and then set up a jack-roll (hand winch) with a wire rope, 120 yards long. Harry recalled:

> It might take a couple of days to do this. Three men held a handle of the jack-roll and three men took hold of the other handle. The remaining man (often me!) had to go down the shaft to investigate and clean out the drainage system. I'd sit on a piece of wood fastened to the wire rope with a safety catch...

When a man stationed below reported on the approach of a train, all Harry could do was to close his mouth and eyes to keep out the smoke:

> Sometimes the smoke took a long time to clear. As it made its way to the tunnel ends or via the ventilation shafts another train would come along—and blow it back again.

## Rise Hill Tunnel

Rise Hill Tunnel, also known as Black Moss, unites the Dent Valley with Garsdale. Its length is 1,213 yards. Remote from roads and villages, the workmen had accommodation provided by the contractors. Men used a tramway that was three-quarters of a mile in length. They sat on bogies and were hauled up from Garsdale by steam engine. The tramway also carried coal, railway material, and provisions.

The Rise Hill Tunnel was driven through blue limestone for 1,213 yards. Excavated hillside material—little more than slush in places—adhered to the implements like treacle. From an engineering point of view, the tunnel was as notable as the celebrated Blea Moor. The deepest of the shafts attained 147 feet. About two-thirds of the arching was of brick and stone—the rest was solid rock. At intervals, the arching was strengthened by iron ribs. There were special problems, including difficulty in access and the need, at great expense, to use a number of wrought-iron supporting ribs, which were tied with rods.

During the construction of Rise Hill tunnel, F. S. Williams, who wrote a good deal about the Settle–Carlisle, descended a shaft in an iron skip and observed 'dimly-burning candles, uncouth-looking wagons standing on the rails or moving to and fro with their numerous lights like twinkling stars in a hazy night'. The noise of twirling drills could be heard beneath the terrible force of big hammers wielded by stalwart men. He would remember 'the *hac hac,* or half sepulchral grunt at each stroke, the murky vapour, the chilling damp and the thick breathing…'

Harry Cox considered that Rise Hill was not as bad as the one under Blea Moor. In the construction period there was slow progress in the cutting to the south of the tunnel because the hillside was breaking away. Excavated material, classified as slurry (slush), was removed with the help of grafting tools and water buckets. The slurry stuck to the tools like treacle! Harry recalled:

> The ganger in my time was George Fawcett, who was also a Wesleyan local preacher. He'd be preaching in the chapel on Sunday when he'd spot Jim Atkinson, one of his men. Breaking off from reading the Bible or preaching, he'd say: 'Tunnel in the morning, Jim. Think on!'

Harry also recalled for me when 'a gang of us', under Tommy Preston, painted the rails:

> Three or four men went ahead, washing the rails. We followed, painting them red to preserve them. Joss Riley was cook for a while. He knocked off work at 11 a.m., an hour before us, and went to the cabin. Outside were wicker baskets, holding our food. Joss took out anything that had to be warmed. It would be ready for us when we knocked off for dinner at noon.

## Birkett Tunnel

What was revered as the Burleigh Rock Drill was used with good effect in Birkett Tunnel. The drill was known to make a hole a foot deep in five minutes. If two men had been working on the same job it would take them forty minutes. In the southern end of Birkett Tunnel, above

Mallerstang, workmen exposed a fine vein of lead ore, and in 1876 a company were driving levels underneath the railway to work it out. The tunnel, hewn for 424 yards, was provided with a brick arch ring throughout.

## Crosby Garrett and Helm Tunnel

Crosby Garrett tunnel was cut through solid rock—a mixture of limestone and grit. The rock was mixed with flint at the heading, within 20 yards of the south entrance. The tunnel was to have a length of 176 yards. From the nature of the rock it was necessary to line the tunnel throughout with brick. Helm Tunnel, near Ormside, was completed in February 1873. The entrances to the tunnel were faced with freestone from a quarry in the neighbourhood. All 600 yards of tunnel were brilliantly illuminated when a company of engineers and local people assembled for mutual congratulation.

Joseph Firbank had Contract No. 3. The first locomotive for use on this contract had arrived locally in March 1871, being drawn to its destination at the Firbank works. The weight of the locomotive was 18 tons. Twenty-one horses, moving three abreast, drew it up the steep hill at Appleby. Joseph Firbank was well-respected by his officials, who met each Boxing Day for dinner and entertainment. In 1871, at the Crown and Cushion, Appleby, the company drank the health of Mr Firbank and Mr J. Thostle, his manager.

For work in Edenvale, Fairbank mustered four locomotives, seventeen portable engines and steam cranes, and 500 earth wagons that moved on 2,000 tons of temporary rails. The embankment at Dandry Mire Moss, which was created near Moorcock, was exceptional. A writer in the *Lancaster Guardian* in 1873 noted that the miry state of the ground had given the contractors and managers:

> ...an inconceivable amount of trouble and labour. Tipping went on for over two years. Instead of a solid embankment being formed, the peat yielded to the weight of the filling to such an extent that it rose on each side of the line as a high bank—in some places reaching 15 feet. After more than 250,000 cubic yards had been tipped, the bog would not sustain the weight of the clay and stone used for filling up. It was decided to make a viaduct in the deepest part of the moss. There would be six arches, each of 45-foot span ... The greatest depth was 53 feet and for nearly the whole length it averaged from 45 feet to 50 feet from foundation to the top of the peat. This varied from 5 ft to 15 feet.

Most of it had to be dug out before the embankment, which was to join the viaduct, could be formed.

In the summer of 1875, the Midland directors toured the completed Settle–Carlisle line on 82-lb steel rails, remaining in the same carriage. Readers of the *Westmorland Gazette* were told that the whole of the works were pushed forward with all speed 'now that the weather [was] so favourable'. The men were being allowed to work all the hours they possibly could so that the line would be open for goods or mineral traffic in either July or the first day in August.

On the official opening day, stations along the new line were crowded with folk who cheered loudly as each train passed by. At Carlisle around 50 acres of land were made available for the construction of engine sheds, goods warehouses, cattle docks, and marshalling sidings. The existing joint passenger station was enlarged and remodelled to admit the new traffic.

5

# Days of Steam: Drivers and Firemen

Matthew Kirtley's locomotives, wearing dark green livery, inaugurated the passenger service, drawing Pullman stock that had been imported from America and setting new standards of luxury in train travel. Kirtley was appointed locomotive superintendent of the Midland in 1841, at the tender age of twenty-eight. He held the office for thirty-two years. Ordinary coaches, riding on six-wheeled bogies, on all-steel rails, moved with unaccustomed smoothness.

Third-class passengers, for long the despised section of the rail-travelling public, occupied upholstered seats. Most other railways had coaches with wooden benches. A Kirtley locomotive was said to be able to do everything but talk. One shortcoming was a Spartan cab; it offered the footplate men little protection against wind and rain. A second disadvantage on such a gruelling route as the Settle–Carlisle was the smallness of this type of loco. Trains had to be double-headed. The Derby 4 loco had a boiler pressure of about 180 lb. Larger engines, such as the Black 5s and the Class 8 freights, had a larger firebox and 225 lb boiler pressure.

Drivers and firemen varied in size and temperament, but were bound together by the spirited response that was needed to operate trains along the 72-mile long railway linking North Ribblesdale with the Eden Valley.

Some footplate men were native-born and spoke local dialect. One man, asked for the time of day, said, 'Yen [one] o'clock, young feller, me lad.' Family pride was detectable. A driver remarked, 'My mother had three of us on t'railway. We were on different shifts, so t'table at home was never cleared of food. Mum had three lots of packing-up. Sandwiches, of course.'

On a steam locomotive, nobody used the word 'stop'. A driver or fireman would shout 'Whoa!' as though he was addressing a horse. A footplate man told me, 'Shout whooooa—and bang goes the brake!' Steam rose to work valves which were connected to the wheels via rods and big-ends. Coal, burnt in a firebox, gave off gases that passed through tubes that were surrounded by water. The heated water became steam, which rose to the top of the locomotive and to the regulator valve, under its distinctive dome. Injectors transferred water from the tender to the boiler. Gauge glasses enabled the footplate men to check on the amount of water in reserve.

A Midland engine driver usually started his railway career cleaning a locomotive. He would progress to the status of fireman and then, many trips later, if all went well, he became a driver. A difference between the drivers of passenger and goods trains was reflected in their wages; at the edge of human memory, a driver on goods got 5 *s* 6 *d* per day. A driver on a passenger trains received the top rate, which was £7 a week.

A knocker-up went on his doleful rounds of the railwaymen's homes twixt 11 p.m. and 7 a.m. He had a book containing the names of the men and details of their duties. 'You used to give a good rap on the door, and t'chap inside would rap at the window. You'd pass on your message, and that was it.' Before a bike was provided, the knocker-up had to walk. There might be a mile between two calls. In a place like Hellifield, the knocking-up process was handy; the railway owned a terrace where many of the railmen lived.

At work, things did not always go according to routine. An old chap who spent years on the footplate of Settle–Carlisle locomotives remarked:

> Sometimes we were so short of steam we had to stop and get steamed-up again. We just couldn't go any farther. If you were near a signal box, you told the signalman. If you weren't, you didn't.

A goods guard recalled when, in the late 1930s, there were lots of shunts. Skipton had a shortage of firemen:

> The blokes they used were fairly young. Sometimes they didn't know enough about the rail route. A young fireman from York had not kept a large enough fire. As they passed the Hoffman kiln at Langcliffe, one driver drew attention to the lofty chimney and said: 'Summit o' t'Settle–Carlisle is about level wi' t'top o' yon chimla.' The lad began shovelling like mad.

The 'coal road' at Settle was for the benefit of five coal merchants. They dealt with domestic coal and also with coke. Industrial fuel was received for Hector Christie and Settle Gas Company, who between them accounted for most of the coal wagons. Smaller quantities were delivered to Settle Rural District Council, Giggleswick School, and Settle Farmers. John Delaney, who sustained a local limestone industry, had a great many wagons. The Settle station yard also held wagons marked 'Charles John Lord' and 'Jim Capstick'. They paid the railway company for wagon-handling.

Goods traffic became common. A loco driver, with a goods train in mind, reported for duty, oiled the side rods, and checked the moving parts of the engine.

> In the case of a freight train bound for Carlisle and Scotland, it might have coke for Rutherglen, wagons full of potatoes or other sorts of merchandise. You backed on to the train, the guard told you the tonnage—and away you went.

One of the footplate men remarked, 'Anyone who got an attack of "tired-itis" didn't care much for the Carlisle road. They used to lie in and come late for work. If you missed your job, the spare man went.'

I heard from the driver of a goods train that the art was keeping up enough steam from Settle to Ais Gill. There was satisfaction in the crew if they went from Leeds to Carlisle in eight hours:

> We'd be coming up the bank from Settle with an old goods train. We had poor coal, the sort they kept for goods engines. It was soft Dearne Valley rubbish. Shovel the stuff into a wagon and it would crumble. It was mucky stuff.
>
> If you stopped for ten minutes your fire was in a mess. You reached for the rake.

I loved to hear the anecdotes of footplate men. One of them remarked:

> At Long Preston you picked up speed and tightened the couplings, then the distant signal for Settle Junction came into view. Wham! Straight off! Unburnt coal flew from the chimney. The fireman kept an eye on the signals. A driver was not expected to cross the cab to look for them yet when he had passed his examination as a driver he was told never to accept the fireman's word that a signal was clear. An old-time semaphore signal could be in somebody's back yard, high up on a post or—as one man told me—round the corner! When you were working on the 'Carlisle road' you were looking all over the place...

The goods office at Settle was small and cramped, measuring not much more than 3 yards by 5 yards. Most of the floor space was taken up by a desk that was double-sided and sloping. It had been painted brown at some time but went piebald after many years of use. Four small windows, two on each side of the office, were kept permanently shut. Cobwebs hung from the ceiling and walls. The Goods Shed had a 'road' through it. The goods were stored on the 'bench'. There were five doors—and not one of them was shut until after the Second World War.

A man born and reared in Carlisle began work on the Settle–Carlisle in 1941. At seventeen years of age, his job was a cleaner. He was promoted to being a footplate man. What made a good fireman? I was told by a seasoned chap:

> He sits with his eyes fixed on the chimney top ... There should just be a haze above it. As soon as it clears it is ready for some more coal. If you don't put some coal on within half a minute, then your steam comes down.

He paused, then:

> As soon as you see your chimney fire clear, you drop the bottom door...

A Carlisle man, a fireman on the Midland route, reckoned that he 'shifted between four and five tons of coal' between the city and Leeds.

How hard the fireman worked depended on the type of locomotive and how big a load you had. If he was 'firing' a Jubilee that was hauling an express, the beat of the loco was such that—as a fireman remarked—'it put it into the atmosphere quicker than you could put it into the firebox'. Nearly every goods train on the Drag was loose-coupled; it called for much experience and skill to keep the couplings tight. When going downhill, the guard applied the handbrake of his van. It was said that some guards kept marbles in a matchbox which they placed on the seat beside them. When the marbles moved to the far end of the box, the train was going downhill. If they rolled towards him, the train was climbing. A guard applied his brake on or off, whichever way he wanted.

Footplate men on the freight trains who had lodged at Carlisle returned to Leeds with countryside produce—with rabbits or eggs bought at certain signal boxes. Crosby Garrett was a good place for getting rabbits:

> On our way back to Leeds, in wartime, we'd look out for pairs of rabbits dangling from the railings of the signal box. They were for sale at 2 *s* 6 *d* the pair. The fireman dampened down the fire, then leapt off the

> locomotive and sprinted to the signal box, running up the steps. The signalman had his hands on the bells; he did not see the visitor nor did he want to know anything about him. In those days, everything was strictly point-to-point timing.

One of the fallacies of the Steam Days is that the footplate men cooked their meals on the fire as the train went happily on its way—they were inclined to gulp down sandwiches. They kept a bottle or can of tea warm on a Derby engine by placing it on a loop formed of pipes that supplied steam to the sanding gear:

> People imagine you had a great big roaring fire on which you cooked bacon and egg. It's a bit of a myth. If you had a shovel and you put bacon on it and shoved it into the firebox when it was red-hot, your bacon would go *whew!* And your eggs with it!

In wintertime, some drivers wore one or two top coats and a muffler. They had caps pulled well down over their ears. As a fireman, Bill Addy of Leeds experienced the extremes of temperature. He fired engines while wearing his heavy railway mackintosh.

Shortly before an August midnight, a railwayman received instructions to book on at 12–5 for piloting the Thames-Clyde Express up to Ais Gill. It was 'black dark'. The pilot engine was of the Midland type, with no doors. 'We were there to assist.' The driver on this occasion was Big Bass Telford. Learning that firing was a novel experience for the newcomer, Big Bass said, 'Stand ower theer. Out o' t'road. Hang on. Just keep your eyes open—and if you see a yellow signal shout at me.' At Garsdale, the pilot engine was taken off. 'We dropped into the sidings and went to Garsdale's famous turntable.' Dawn was breaking as they returned to Carlisle.

Holbeck, at Leeds, was the base concerned entirely with the passenger side of the railway. A Holbeck driver got the best of the locos and available coal. He was said to 'go by' with his nose in the air. Coaches were called 'mahoganies'—though what you might take for wood-grain was, indeed, paint of an appropriate hue. 'He's on mahoganies,' a friend of the driver of a passing train might say. If the weather was inclement, the fireman might resign himself to shovelling water into the firebox—and wondering when the train would come to a stand. Goods trains spent much of their time in sidings, letting the passenger trains go through. One driver was in the habit of disappearing from the footplate for forty minutes—you were not likely to be clear in less time. He knew the situation of every lineside pub.

A veteran driver told me that Kingsmoor, a major centre, just north of Carlisle, was busy:

> ...busier than any place I had been in ... You left your engine in the line. It made its way to the ash-pit. There were two rows of engines there—as many as twenty or thirty engines. They were waiting to have their fires cleaned out. We went to book off, then walked to the lodge to have our nine hours off. And as we walked the engine we had left was only just getting on to the ash pit.

Coal and steam! These were the main elements in operating the line. The best coal for the engines came from Yorkshire pits. 'It was a mixed grill, was coal. You couldn't expect anything else. A lot of it was rubbish.' In 1963, when light engines were despatched to Blea Moor for snow-ploughing, they had to clean the fire when they got there. Dirty coal! Yorkshire hards resembled slate in appearance. Hit it with a hammer and it would break up in layers. Put it on a fire in a locomotive—and the coal simply crackled. 'You could see bits flying off it.'

Among the freight engines stabled at Skipton were 'the old Derby 4s'. Each had a small tank. A fireman told me:

> If you had a heavy load, you'd leave Skipton with a full tank and hope to get some more water at Settle. This would take you as far as Blea Moor. After that, you thought of the troughs at Garsdale. You could get some water at Kirkby Stephen, Appleby and so on.

Blea Moor tunnel made a railwayman shiver. A young fireman remarked:

> When you came out of Blea Moor tunnel, the first thing you noticed was the cemetery on your left—gravestones of men who died when the line was being made. You passed through a small cutting and then suddenly crossed Dent Head viaduct. And there was the valley, a long way down. That day we had a Derby 3. There was quite a space between the engine and the tender. When I wasn't shovelling, I swept up to keep the muck down...

Someone in the Eden Valley set up a scarecrow in a field. This was not to discourage birds but to attract the attention of footplate men. A fireman could not resist lobbing cobs of coal at the scarecrow as the train passed. The owner of the field occasionally visited the scarecrow to collect the coal! A guard on a steam train had his own van at the rear. Old-time guards travelled in unheated vans and, in winter, were known to warm their feet on bags of straw; then a stove became the centrepiece. The guard sometimes created a Catherine-wheel effect when he had applied the brakes too hard.

In January 1980, British Railways permitted the start of regular steam excursions over the Settle–Carlisle line—though it was then under notice of closure. The special train was initially known as the *Cumbrian Mountain Express*. A set of Pullman coaches, bought from BR, resulted in that change of name. The train operated in 'two legs'. A special train, which was to travel northwards, was taken over by a steam locomotive at Carnforth. One engine would haul the train to Skipton (or, from 1981, to Hellifield) where another was waiting to haul the train up to Ais Gill Summit (1,169 feet), then down the verdant Eden Valley to Carlisle. A week later the same run was repeated in reverse direction.

6

# Signal Boxes: Especially Remote Blea Moor

Signalmen are among the unsung heroes of the Settle–Carlisle. For well over a century, their working life has been solitary. At the most remote boxes, on winter nights, the only sound between trains was the hiss of a paraffin lamp or the creaking of timbers being tormented by a Pennine gale. Before the First World War, a signalman was expected to wear a collar and tie when on duty. These were kept in a locker and hurriedly donned when an inspector was seen to be approaching the box.

## Settle Junction

Until the 1930s, all boxes were fitted with telegraph instruments. For a time, from 1874, Settle Junction had two signal boxes. The South Box controlled the switching of traffic from the north to the Morecambe line. It was renewed in 1894 and removed in 1922. A fence composed of sleepers was erected between the railway and the Keighley-Kendal road; the barrier was installed so that horses would not be scared by the sight of passing trains.

## Settle

Settle was described to me as 'a lovely little box to work in'. I used to pop in when Mr Carter was on duty. He was a signalman and also a devout chapelgoer, which is where I met him. The signal box was a busy place. Each day, on average, a train passed Settle every twenty minutes:

> Then you had one or two different shunts. There'd maybe a train of cattle wagons staying here for a week. People took 'em as they wanted them. Settle had a full-time shunter.

Dick Clarke, who for many years served in the signal box at Helwith Bridge, was startled by the sound of a chain being rattled. He eventually plucked up courage to wander out of the box. A collie dog had broken away from its kennel. The chain had caught between the capstones of a wall it had attempted to leap. The dog was striving to free itself. When some wagons containing explosives broke free of a train and clattered down a track, Dick—learning about it by phone—dashed to a corner of the sloping field. The trucks rattled merrily by, coming to a halt near Settle Junction.

## Blea Moor

My favourite signal box is Blea Moor, standing beside the Settle–Carlisle railway to the south of Blea Moor. The box is not one of the familiar Midland style. In the early part of the Second World War the layout of the tracks had been changed from back-in sidings to loops. The box was replaced by one of the late-LMS period in which the levers are closer together. There is a left-hand frame. The signalman, when working the levers, faces the back wall instead of looking directly through the front windows.

Nearby were relatively modern dwellings for railwaymen. Most signalmen walked or cycled to work, leaving a road at Ribblehead and progressing on a track adjacent to the railway lines. They reported for duty at what, in steam days, was a busy box, set in a moorland wilderness. The toilet at Blea Moor box was a small cubicle adjoining the steps used to gain entry to the controls. A signalman remarked, 'It wasn't ower safe in a reet strong wind. I've heard of one toilet takking off—with a feller still sat there!'

The box containing the toilet at Blea Moor was of the Elsan type, set at the top of the steps. A signalman mentioned to me that 'you just went out of the door and turned to t'reet, and it was there'. The duty signalman at Blea Moor box rarely lacked company. A ganger and his merry men would hand over tins of food with the request that they might be warmed up by noon. One man laughed when one batch of tins was collected. He mentioned to the signalman, who had heaped all the tins on the stove, that it would be the first time he ate boiled pears.

Other callers were locomotive crews waiting to change trains, members of special duty gangs, and railway enthusiasts. Among them was Eric

Treacy, who was known as The Railway Bishop. He had a special love for the Blea Moor box. Also calling at the box after dark were walkers who had been lost on the fells. I have listened to a few Settle–Carlisle ghost stories, but most of the strangest tales might be classified as 'strange happenings'.

George Horner was a good friend I met at the Blea Moor box or in his home at Horton-in-Ribblesdale. He recalled the day when a sheep was lying in the four-foot, between the tracks, chewing her cud placidly. When an inspector arrived at the box he insisted that the signalman should 'get her off'; she was in danger. The signalman replied, 'It's her blooming look-out if she gets run over.' A train was offered and accepted. The inspector told George he couldn't bear to watch it, but George couldn't resist and turned to look at her:

> In a bit, there was a rumbling and t'big yellow nose of t'express could be seen as it came under t'bridge. Sheep was still there.... Just as t'express was passing, yon sheep got up, stretched and walked out o' t'way. The express shot by her at high speed. The sheep languidly returned to the place where she had been—and lay down again.

Blea Moor box crackled and creaked during a strong wind. George was glad he was not of the nervous type because when he heard the steps creaking on a windy day he had no idea whom it might be. He once produced a ghost-like sound for a couple of walkers who were wandering about—lost. Said George, 'They went off like the wind.'

Everyone who visited Blea Moor box remembered the stove and the kettle, which had a song in its heart throughout the twenty-four hours. George told me, 'In the old days we had what we called Russell stoves; they had a coal fire and an oven above. We would get a good fire going underneath and put the kettle in the oven.' Blea Moor was a changeover point for loco men. Gallons of tea were drunk.

The denizens of the two houses that stood near the signal box burnt coal and peat in the grates, some of the coal being large pieces dropped off the tenders of passing trains by firemen who did not fancy breaking them up. Generally, it was hard and brittle coal which, when glowing, was almost capable of melting the grate. The toilet at a railway cottage was a small building at the back.

## Selside

Until the 1930s, all the signal boxes on the Settle–Carlisle had telegraph instruments. Selside was the only main line signal box manned round the clock by women. 'There was no cross-over road, nothing of any intricacy about it—just two levers one way and two levers t'other way.'

One time, when Albert Wilson was signalman, the box was nearly taken from under him. The box was held up by the back wall; 'There was a lot o' cant on the curve at Stainforth, you know, and there were also sidings for Craven Quarry.' The lofty chimney at a Hoffman Kiln was said to attain the same elevation as Ais Gill summit. Helwith Bridge and Horton boxes also dealt with a good deal of quarry traffic.

## Stainforth and Helwith Bridge

'A signalman was witness to some dramatic events.' Stainforth box, at the junction with a limestone quarry, was not popular. It was a simple, easy little box. The man in charge feared a derailment. It had happened twice; wagons left the tracks and collided with it. On the second incident, the upper storey was left dangling from the extra-strong back wall of the box. This incident led to a local man suggesting that it should be provided with an ejector seat. When a signalman at Helwith Bridge was notified about a runaway train, he did not remain on duty in the box but fled up the field. On another occasion, a train was halted and for several hours men searched the lines and the countryside round about for a missing man. He was located, hale and hearty, at a local inn.

## Dent

At Dent, the electricity used for working the signal box was stored in batteries. The first of these were glass jars with water, white tablets, and zinc. Dry batteries were used at a later date, being maintained by men from Settle. This signal box was small, with three signals each way and a cross-over road. The duty man reached the box via field footpath from the road. Some of the men who worked there came from Ribblehead via Blea Moor. If they were 'pushed' for time they might even go through Blea Moor tunnel—a dangerous experience.

If there was sometimes a longish gap in between nocturnal trains the signalman was tempted to take a cat-nap. 'This was not wise. He might fall into a deep sleep.' Some men had ways of keeping themselves awake. One signalman donned his hat and coat and sat on the veranda. Another played his violin. Quite a few signalmen kept up lengthy telephone conversations with pals in the adjoining signal boxes.

At Dent box, the signalman might receive and despatch postal messages. A cycle was provided for their delivery. During a thunderstorm in the

1930s, the signalman observed a remarkable incident. A 'thunderbolt' fell at the door of the platelayers' cabin on the up-line side, which was quite near the signal box. In the box a blue flame or light seemed to run the length of the instrument shelf. There was a faint jingle of bells and also a smell of sulphur. Returning to the box, the signalman discovered that most of the instruments had been affected.

## Ormside

Signal men were known to have additional jobs—'bits o' sidelines'. Some men caught and sold rabbits. A Grizeburn man whittled away making sticks and shepherds' crooks. Frank Ridding, at Ormside, made some 'extra brass' as a cobbler and got an allocation of leather during the war for mending shoes. The old drivers would come from Leeds, slinging a pair of shoes off as they were going by. There'd be a little note such as 'Back on the 10-55'. Frank would set to work and repair the shoes in time to hand them back. The driver would stop and pick them up; it cost 12 *s* 6 *d* for soling and heeling.

In the 1950s, when railwaymen were not particularly well-paid, a few extra pounds a month came in handy where a man had a large and growing family. One signalman joyously proclaimed, 'I've done it!' With much overtime, he had that week drawn £10 in his wage packet.

Signal boxes were usually warm and snug. Enter one—unofficially—and you might find a kettle on the stove, singing away, and almost ready for the mashing of tea. One updale signalman, who was familiar with the Russell type of stove, said:

> It had a coal fire at t'bottom and an oven on top. You could get a good fire underneath and put t'kettle in t'oven. It was possible to cook owt in a signal box. I'd a mate who made jam and bottled fruit.

The Russell stoves were eventually replaced by a simple stove that lacked an oven.

Endless tales were told by my old railway friends about the signal boxes on the Settle–Carlisle. The box at Settle Junction was especially active on a summer's day. In the 1950s, fifteen to twenty trains went to Morecambe alone. The junction at Hellifield was also excessively busy—a signalman might deal with over 100 trains in eight hours.

Lots of fascinating stories were told about the signal box at Blea Moor. George Horner, full of tales of Settle–Carlisle in the past, recalled in particular the night shifts he kept at Blea Moor box. George had to be on duty for 10 p.m. He said:

> Unless there was a brilliant moonlit night—which, of course, you did get from time to time—you needed a torch. If you were on from 2 till 10 you'd see your mate coming to relieve you. You'd see his light coming over t'hill.

One night there were some unexpected visitors—ramblers who had lost their way in the dark. They entered the box. George said, teasingly, 'We have some ghosts around here. Every now and again the door blows open, and there stands a friendly ghost. He doesn't harm anybody.' The ramblers had arrived on a breezy night. George recalled, 'The door broke open. Next time I looked, the walkers were running away.'

Typically, a signalman at Blea Moor box regarded his task with levity and humour. He referred to the tunnel as 'The Toob'. A signalman-cum-hairdresser got much custom from crews waiting, at the box, for the arrival of trains from Carlisle, when they would exchange places with the Carlisle men. One evening, just after haytime, a driver heard a clomping on the step, and into the box came six farmhands. Each had hair that was so long they resembled hillbillies; the signalman set to work cutting it. The visiting driver swept it up to keep the box clean.

During the Second World War an ammunition train broke in two at Blea Moor. Thirty vans were seen by signalmen as they hurtled down the tracks. The guard of the train noted that his efforts were of no avail, and leapt clear. He was later informed that the vans had come to a halt at Long Preston, about 16 miles from the point where they had broken loose.

One evening, after snow had fallen, a signalman headed for a term of duty at Selside box (which has since been taken away and is an exhibit at Steamtown, Carnforth). The signalman trudged in fresh snow from Horton to Selside. The road conditions had been too bad for him to use his car. As he neared the signal box, he saw a man who had been walking towards it unexpectedly turn away to cross the railway lines. George, reaching the snowy area frequented by that man, could not locate a single footprint!

Jack Sedgwick, a special Dentdale friend of mine, was a signalman at high-lying Dent, where signals had frequently to be cut out of lofty snowdrifts. Jack divided his time between signalman and hairdresser, using the box as a salon. He had some celebrated visitors; Bishop Treacy called. He was wearing an ordinary tie, and not a clerical collar. It was not the Bishop's first visit. Jack said, 'He enjoyed listening to Dent box talk afore t'men found out he wor a parson.' This signal box was made redundant. A sad-faced Jack recalled, 'T'woodwork was put to the torch.'

To reach the Mallerstang box, a signalman travelled to the area by motorbike, leaving his machine in Outhgill churchyard and then trudging up a hillside. When his turn was due to begin on a moonless night, he could not always find the wall-stiles; 'I had to clamber over the wall-tops ... When the weather was really bad, I'd to wait for the passing of the next train to let me know I was going in the right direction.'

There was no water supply in the Mallerstang box. 'It was suggested that I went "up the line" for water—which I did. I found a wee stream.' The relief signalman, after being told where he had found water, shook his head and said, 'You should have gone to the next stream. There's a dead hoss [horse] lying a bit further up the hillside from the first one.'

All was not lost when Settle signal box closed in 1984. It lay in a derelict state until 1996 when the Friends of Settle–Carlisle volunteers moved it to a point closer to the station and restored it to its former glory. It is now open on Saturdays and special occasions. Visitors have an opportunity of operating the old-time equipment, covering the process of an imaginary train. There is a framed photograph of Derek Soames, who spent most of his working life at the signal box situated at Settle Junction.

# 7

# The Stations: Local Stone, Gothic Style

Stations were usually faced with stone and had steeply-pitched roofs. Three sizes of station were brought into use. The largest size was selected for Settle, Kirkby Stephen, and Appleby. John Holloway Sanders (1826–1884), the Midland's architect, designed the Settle–Carlisle stations. These designs—for large, medium, and small structures—became known as Derby or Midland Gothic, and the handiest building materials were used. At the southern end of the line, considerable quantities of stone came from quarries in Bradford. Limestone was commonly used on stations beside the Long Drag. The Eden Valley sprouted stations made from quarried, rose-red sandstone.

A vital feature of a station platform in the 'steam days' was the water column. It has a cast-iron outer casing and a steel pipe within. It was inclined to freeze at the neck, the place where the pipe could be swivelled over the tender of a locomotive. In frosty weather I remember seeing a brazier in place. A Settle man told me that the fire did not always clear the ice. The station staff was inclined, unofficially, to wrap cotton waste around the neck, soak the waste with paraffin—and put a match to it! The water supply for the column at Settle flowed from Stainforth in a lineside channel.

## Hellifield

Hellifield, a junction to the south of Settle, throbbed with railway life. The Lancashire and Yorkshire Railway (Lanky) took advantage of the

Settle–Carlisle route by providing it with a link across the border. L&Y locomotives had a black livery, which was relieved by red and white banding. In January 1922, the railway company was absorbed by the London and North Western Railway. A year later it was owned by LMS—the London Midland and Scottish Railway Company.

An influx of railway workers and their families led to a trebling of Hellifield's population, and by 1931 over 1,000 people were to be found here. Harry Speight, the late Victorian topographer, had written:

...the rather elevated and windy position of the station on the edge of Hellifield Moor is not calculated to 'jubilate' the traveller on a raw night. There is, however, ample waiting room accommodation, a bookstall and a refreshment room. I remember the latter very well. On a chill day in winter it was good to be in a space heated by a large coal fire. I was present when one of the railwaymen came in with another bucket of coal.

Hellifield was, indeed, shift-conscious. The station blazed with light all night long. In the wee small hours a knocker-up made his doleful rounds, rapping on the doors of railwaymen—driver, fireman, guard—and shouting official instructions such as 'double head to Carlisle'. The person being 'knocked up', with sleep still on his eyes, would acknowledge the call by tapping the inside of the bedroom window.

My old friend Jimmy Fishwick had worked in the engine shed, which had three 'roads' for trains, office, and heavy equipment—firebricks and bars—that were spare. He was to pass through a trio of grades—cleaner, fireman, and then driver.

Jimmy and his friends removed the fire from a locomotive, then waited for it to cool down before they could enter the firebox to clean the tube-ends. Several grades of coal were available. An inferior type, allocated to engines hauling goods trains, came in long, brittle cobs and was nicknamed 'legs and arms'. The choice coal, known as Yorkshire Main, was available for passenger trains.

James Richardson, who took up residence in 1921, saw the start of a building boom which had soon doubled the village in size; he remarked, 'I would say that at least half the people in the village were railwaymen. The whole place seemed to work on a shift system.' Midland Terrace (40 houses) and L&Y Terrace had been built by the railway companies for their workers.

Hellifield, in the old steam times, was a bustling place, active for twenty-four hours a day. A branch line to Lancashire is still open. The engine shed, which was closed in 1963, once held twenty-five locomotives, including those that had been brought here for repair. A man called O'Hare started the Hellifield Railway Mission. W. H. Smith erected the bookstall in 1901; it was replaced in 1907 by a structure that was used until its closure in 1956.

Jimmy had become a full-time engine driver for British Railways in 1947. He was soon familiar with the Settle–Carlisle line. Jimmy, training on diesels, met a driver from Hull who, after traversing this line, said, 'Do you know—if I'd been made a fireman over this road I would have given in my notice.' There were, however, some moist local eyes among the Hellifield men when steam was withdrawn from the Drag. To Jimmy Fishwick and his contemporaries, there was something special about the Days of Steam.

## Settle

Settle was provided with a station when J. Thornton, a Bradford builder, tendered successfully for its construction at the edge of town. He used gritstone from the Bradford area, with the addition of fretted bargeboards. Platform stone came from Shipley. Level ground for the station was created by tipping a vast amount of material from the Ingfield area. It was rested against massive retaining walls.

Anyone who strolls along the 'down' platform and looks over the wall has the impression of being on the bulwarks of a castle. The extended platforms are connected by an iron footbridge brought here from Drem, in the North East. Those who cross the bridge have a superb view of the local landscape, including Giggleswick Scars.

Porters had a hectic round in the 1930s. At Settle, the first train of the day, at 6.20 a.m., was the workman's to Horton-in-Ribblesdale. On Saturday, the first train was the 7.20 a.m. to Leeds; the last train at night being the 10.30 to Leeds. In 1934, a man who took up work as a 'domestic porter' received £2 a week, but the take-home pay was 37 *s*.

When gas was the method of illuminating the station, each lamp had a pilot light and 'you pulled a chain each evening to light the mantle'. The light would be turned off when the last train had departed and the duty porter was about to go home. If he was halfway between one platform light and another, he would be in almost total darkness. The really important lamps were those at either end of the platform; they marked its limits and were used by train drivers arriving after dark.

*Wildman's Almanac*, published at Settle in 1874, noted that the new station had a station house, a house for the stationmaster, a large goods warehouse, a water tank for supplying the engines, and a weigh house. A large goods warehouse was constructed. It was capable of accommodating five trucks at once. I recall it in its later days when it was just an empty shell. There had been platforms for unloading cattle, carriages, and horses.

Israel Horton, through his foreman, James Gray, attended to the construction of a Stationmaster's House, the goods shed, and the stonework supporting the main water tank. The Midland style of decoration was known to the staff as 'plum and straw'. Settle station once had a thriving goods department, with a coal 'road' and cattle pens. Five coal merchants had their huts beside the 'coal road'. The Settle staff handled such varied products as cattle feed, corn, wheat, barley, straw, hay, farm machinery and, in season, wool from local sheep.

Trains were available for workmen commuting to Mr Delaney's limestone quarry at Horton-in-Ribblesdale. The Tuesday market day at Settle led to station visits by farmers' wives with baskets containing butter and eggs. Eric Middleton, who was twenty-two years old when he began work for the railway, recalled that in 1934 the staff at Settle numbered over thirty people. Eric's wage was £2 per week; with stoppages, the take-home pay was 37 *s*. He paid 25 *s* for local lodgings. It was a time when lodgers were not expected to be in the house over the weekend, so Eric used some of his meagre resources to go home, giving his mother half a crown towards expenses.

Jim Taylor, a well-remembered stationmaster who was first associated with the Settle–Carlisle in 1947, was an efficient railman who is especially remembered for his gardening abilities. He created prize-winning floral plots on the platforms at Settle, the ideas having been first devised when he was at Horton-in-Ribblesdale, where platforms were at an elevation of 850 feet above sea level.

## Horton-in-Ribblesdale

Horton-in-Ribblesdale had an important rail connection with the local limestone quarry. John Delaney, who developed the quarry, was born in Ireland in 1846—a period known to historians as the Hungry Forties. Delaney worked for a time at Christie's Mill in Langcliffe. In adulthood, he exploited limestone on a grand scale, developing quarries at Horton-in-Ribblesdale and Threshfield.

Within fifteen years of his limestone venture, Delaney had made a fortune. He had been aided by John Winskill, who built him a stone kiln at Beecroft. The name of the Horton quarry took its name from that of a farm. Delaney recruited men from Derbyshire and the lime they made available was transported by rail to Sheffield. It helped to meet the needs of the burgeoning steel mills.

The quarry at Horton was active and prosperous for many years after Delaney's death in 1921. The quarry owners dealt annually with 250,000 tons of incoming coal and outgoing lime. The lime was used mainly as a flux in the Scottish steel industry and for surfacing roads.

At Horton, trains with empty trucks had to deliver them up a steep bank. They deliberately overshot the station, and then the train and trucks went into reverse with a high enough speed to storm the incline to the quarry where more limestone awaited them. A man who made a points mistake during the quarry stretch of the line caused he trucks to end their journey 'in the beck'.

Horton had colourful little platform gardens devised, planted, and weeded by the Stationmaster, the aforementioned Jim Taylor. Local flower beds—at Horton and Settle—blazed with colour provided by eye-catching plants. A sundial, set on a plinth of stone taken from nearby Penyghent, was centrepiece of the floral display.

At this time, the waiting room at Horton-in-Ribblesdale had a geological exhibition and also an art and photographic display. Many of the paintings in the former were valuable but uninsured. No painting was damaged or lost. Jim Taylor moved to Settle Station, which was soon to have a floral appeal.

## Ribblehead

Ribblehead Station, 1,000 feet above sea level, is one of the smallest of the three types installed on the Settle–Carlisle. In this wild, wet situation, a modification to the normal Midland style was the addition of tiles to the end and projecting gables. Batty Green, the name first chosen for the station, related to a soggy expanse of ground at the dale head—ground across which, with enormous skill, the huge viaduct was to take shape.

Ribblehead Station had a fine house for the Stationmaster and his family. The house is now owned by a trust who have restored it and made it available to paying visitors. Mike Neal, stationmaster in the first decade of this century, told me that on a wild night he and his wife Rosie could scarcely sleep in that house for the rattling and banging: 'In the morning, we'd go outside to see if any roof slates were missing.'

Wind and rain frequently combined to torment local folk. One day, Mike had to hold on to fencing to avoid being blown over. An evening might be wet and dull. The next morning, the sun, rising over Cam End like a blow-torch, would eventually dip out of sight behind the ponderous form of Whernside.

The ever-changing effect of light and shade on the piers of Ribblehead viaduct was a constant delight to the Neals. In quiet spells they exchanged whistles with visiting birds —chaffinches and titmice. They were attracted by seed placed in a horizontal wire container that had been shaped and painted like a railway locomotive.

In 1953 I paid the first of many visits to Ribblehead Station. It was a time when Ribblehead was also a weather station, valuable because of its high Pennine setting. M. A. Elliot, the stationmaster, sent coded details about the weather to the Air Ministry, assessing the cloud height by releasing a hydrogen-filled balloon and timing its ascent. Ribblehead had become a weather station in 1938, but it was not until 1954 that a rain gauge was installed.

During the first year a bucket would have been appropriate. The annual fall was reckoned at rather more than 109 inches; 5 inches of rain had descended on a single day in December.

At Ribblehead, where several valleys converge, the weather can be turbulent—hence the wry nickname 'Windy Wibblehead'. A westering gale might wail like a banshee as it strums the piers of the railway viaduct. Men stationed at the north end of the viaduct when a gale was forecast had the task of tightening the ropes that held tarpaulins to wagons. A slack tarpaulin might become a windfall in a literal sense for a local farmer.

In the pre-Christmas period, Ribblehead station was the destination for what was termed 'the music train'. The annual evening excursion, from Settle to Ribblehead, included jazz. Those who attended were treated to real ale. When I visited Ribblehead in 1953, about 100 trains a day were clattering up and down the lines, the trains ranging from fast expresses to stopping trains and slow freights.

As I stood near the inn, a roadman—grandson of a couple who worked here when the line was under construction—pointed out the scarcely discernible roads between the huts of one of the long-lost shanty towns created when the line was under construction. The shanty had included, apart from homes and offices, a post office and public library, mission house and hospital, with an isolation ward on a hillock situated on the other side of the road.

## Dent

The railway approached Dent on a ledge cut from the lower slopes of a hill known as Great Knoutberry (which is 2,200 feet high). The road leading to the station is three quarters of a mile long. Some of the station buildings, well-maintained, are now in private hands and available as holiday accommodation. In the old days, I enjoyed visiting Dent station from Garsdale via the old Coal Road leading over the fells to Dent station.

Nature occasionally asserted itself. I recall a winter's day at Dent station when a wilderness effect was completed by a blackcock, 'big as a littleish turkey', which was nonchalantly pecking scarlet berries from a local thorn tree. I had used a four-arch overbridge (no. 96) accommodating the aforementioned Coal Road, so named because it served a number of little bell-pits from which a hard, brittle coal was recovered.

Dent station had not even been finished when the Settle–Carlisle line was open for traffic in May 1876. There had been differences about where it should be placed. One idea was that it might be constructed further south of the present position, and given the name Dent Head. The Reverend D. Adams, parson of Cowgill, suggested to the company that the name should be simply 'Dent'—they agreed. He may have been among the first to hear that hoary tale of the visitor who asked why Dent station should be so far (5 miles) from Dent Town. The reply was, 'Appen they wanted it near t'lines.'

Parson Adams had earlier dealings with the Midland Company. The influx of railway navvies had turned quiet little hamlets like Lea Gate briefly into boom towns. Among the social problems was what to do with the bodies of railway workers who died locally. Those bodies were interred in a specially extended graveyard. A cache of local documents, found in the roof at Dent station in quite recent times, included counterfoils for first-class tickets in 1883. You could travel from Dent to Hawes for 1 *s* 11 *d*; to Blackburn for 7 *s* 2 *d*; to Northallerton for 5 *s* 11 *d*; and to Liverpool for 12 *s* 1 *d*.

The Stationmaster's House at Dent, for long a private residence, was taking shape in the 1870s. It was made on a plan used throughout the Settle–Carlisle system. There was a novel feature; the windows were 'double-glazed', a form of glazing that was inexplicably removed during the Second World War and not replaced. It was exceptional. A Midland architect had arranged to cheat the wind by setting two windows 6 inches apart.

'Marble' from Arten Gill was despatched from Dent to monumental masons in the South. The station waiting room acquired a fireside surround made of this type of polished, fossilised limestone.

In its heyday, Dent dealt with a vast range of goods. In November 1887, a corpse was consigned by rail the 56 miles from Leeds to Dent. The charge was a shilling per mile; it cost the bereaved family £2.80.

When a Lancashire school rented the main building at Dent station, the aforementioned files of old documents were removed from the loft. The documents hinted at the past life at the highest station in the land. In 1896 the staff handled a mowing machine, twenty loads of corn, six bags of sugar, four buckets of lard, and innumerable loads of basic slag in 2-cwt bags.

My old friend Cecil Sanderson, a former stationmaster at Dent who had been born and reared on the Plain of York, revelled in the high life. He had a novel way of sealing the house against draughts; in the depths of winter, he sprayed it with water from a hosepipe, forming a protective shield of ice. Sandy, as he was called by his friends, said that snow did not fall from above—it was 'lateral snow', with ice and hailstones mixed in. 'If you were not careful in windy weather, you might be blown off your feet.'

Alexander Frater, in a train journey on the Settle–Carlisle, noted that beyond the viaducts of Dent Head and Arten Gill, the line 'began scoring points, dealing only in superlatives'. The road approach to Dent station from the valley was both memorable and exhausting—a steep climb, with sharp bends lower down. Alfred J. Brown considered:

> ...it is a mistake to rush up that steep road to Dent station hard on the heels of breakfast ... it plays havoc with one's lungs and digestion; yet in spite of the wheezing and groaning, how rich the reward as one tops the rise!

## Garsdale Head

Garsdale Head, 22 miles from Settle station, stands at the northern end of what generations of railway loco-men called The Long Drag. When I visited the station towards the close of 1972, it looked forlorn, having been stripped of almost all the Victorian grandeur—and also, in 1959, the branch line connecting Settle–Carlisle with the Wensleydale line.

Winds strummed Garsdale at a velocity that attained 100 miles per hour. A signalman at the Garsdale box frequently felt his chair moving under him. Garsdale turntable was ringed by a timber stockade. In 1900, when a gale blew furiously, a locomotive on the turntable spun like a top—for two hours. Progress became slower as sand was tipped into the central well. The turntable was eventually made obsolete; it was removed several years before the end of steam haulage.

Trains arriving at Garsdale brought livestock. There were docks for cattle and horses, and pens for sheep. Mr Bell Pratt went into Scotland for cows and local farmers collected them from the station or employed a drover. The cattle usually came into Garsdale on a late train and Tommy walked them through the night. Garsdale handled cattle, sheep, and even horses from Middleham that were en route to race meetings.

An old lady who occupied a cottage recalled for me that often, during the night, she would hear a rumbling sound as Scotch animals acquired by the Pratt family were driven from the wagons into the dock to await attention. If Scottish cattle arrived during the day, they would be driven down the road known as Shop Hill. Children were terrified when they saw cows with great long horns. A vast number of Scottish sheep that were borne to Garsdale by special train were unloaded and let out on Garsdale Common.

Mr Bell Pratt had an early-morning ride in horse and trap, controlled by a lady relative, to catch a train at Garsdale, from which station he was transported to a cattle sale in Scotland. Local farmers collected animals from the station or employed a drover like Tommy Byker, of Gayle, to deliver them. The cattle usually arrived at Garsdale on a late train. Tommy walked them through the night.

A remarkable lady living at Hawes recalled when she used to drive her father in a horse-drawn trap to the Garsdale station (often called The Junction). Dad was a cattle dealer, heading for Scotland. Once she was rather late and simply threw a coat over her nightdress. There was hardly any road traffic at that time. On the return journey, a kind old lady living at a roadside cottage brought the horse and trap to a halt and made her a cup of tea.

Garsdale had a battered old register containing a list of lost property dating back to 1895. In that year a whip and a retriever dog were found without their owners. The entries for the following year mentioned a basket of rhubarb and a parcel of clogs. On the page headed 1923 was written: 'tin box containing bits of linseed cake' and 'three ploughshares'.

In 1971, spending a day chatting with local folk, I heard that some had counted between seventy and eighty trains a day. Porters at Garsdale clambered along the roofs of carriages if the gas jets in the compartments were to be lit. When the Garsdale to Hawes junction ceased to exist, the Wensleydale line was ripped up.

Memories remained of *Bonnyface*, the Hawes-Bradford train. Some people said the train had been nicknamed after a particularly ugly permanent way inspector; others thought it had a bonny face when platelayers, seeing the smoke box of the returning train glinting in the evening light, knew their day's work was almost over. It was the bonniest face they saw during their shift. John Mason of Hawes, who started to work for the railway as a lad porter in 1900, told me that one of his duties, at 5.45 a.m., was to fill the foot-pans that provided warmth for the compartments of passenger trains. The job took an hour and a half.

The 2-mile length of the gang at Garsdale included the famous water troughs, which lay to the south of the station. Nearly all the expresses coming up The Long Drag had their scoops lowered, just to the north of Rise Hill, to collect water at the troughs, a situation chosen because it was the only piece of line that was appropriately straight and level. The dimensions of the troughs (which were installed in 1907 at a cost of £4,396) were impressive—a length of 1,670 feet and a water capacity of between 5,000 and 6,000 gallons, about a third of which might be taken up by a thirsty locomotive. A trough was deep in the middle and shallow at each end.

The troughs were fed by water from a moor-edge reservoir that flowed to a lineside storage tank, which could hold 43,000 gallons. A liquid mixture composed of several ingredients was drip-fed into the tank to keep the water clean and free-running. One element in the water softened it. Another element, known as 'boiler tan', stopped the interior of the boiler from rusting. Thirdly, an anti-foam substance prevented frothing.

The troughs were indicated to an approaching train-driver by a white cross in a black box, the source of the light being a paraffin lamp. When the cross came into sight, the loco-scoop was dipped. If the train was double-headed, an agreement had to be reached. 'You took one half and t'driver of the other loco took the other half.' About a third might be taken up by a single locomotive in a few dramatic moments.

Collecting water at the Garsdale troughs involved split-second timing. The scoop had to be wound down into the troughs at a precise time. If the night was pitch-black—or there were lightless wartime conditions—a train driver counted bridges. In warm weather, the guard walked from carriage to carriage asking passengers to keep the windows closed! If the water at the troughs had frozen, a locomotive driver on the 'down' time would have to make a stop for water at Appleby.

In winter, workmen spent much time picking ice from between trough and rail. The ice had to be kept below rail level or there could be a train off the road. We had a cabin with a fire spot where we could have our meals. There was always plenty of coal that had been washed off the engines using the troughs. If the tank was overfull, water poured out and washed cobs of coal off the tender. It could be a dangerous job; lids were supposed to be chained down, but sometimes there were no chains. The lids flew everywhere.

In the 1950s, the troughs were removed for maintenance. A few years later they were taken up and sent for scrap.

In 1938, a visitor to Garsdale with time to spare might go into the waiting room. J. F. Ferguson, the stationmaster, would almost certainly lend him or her one of 150 books kept in a library. At the turn of the century these books had been presented by two elderly ladies from Wensleydale who travelled via Garsdale—or Hawes Junction, as it then was known. Douglas Cobb made interesting changes when, in 1953, he became stationmaster at Garsdale. Hearing that two drinking fountains had been removed, he introduced the idea of a platform garden, importing the soil and placing it on platforms which, at around 1,000 feet in elevation, were swept by bitter winds.

I saw the Tank House when it was being demolished. From about the end of the First World War until the coming of television diverted attention, Garsdalians had used the Tank House as a centre for domino and whist drives, potato-pie suppers, and concerts. Dancing was popular. The 'wallflowers' sat on red-upholstered seats taken from a scrapped railway carriage. The buffet was a wheel-less railway carriage of Midland ancestry, sporting the original doors.

## Ormside

The Settle–Carlisle had a change of character in the Eden Valley. The Valley is vast, fanning out into a plain when close to Solway Firth. The scenery beside the dramatic Eden Gorge—with its heather and pinewoods—has affinities with the Scottish Highlands. Ormside, high up the vale, lost its halts by passenger trains in 1952. Ormside Viaduct marked the first crossing of the Eden. One of the 90-foot-high, stone-built piers had its feet in water. The arches of this splendid viaduct were lined with bricks.

## Appleby

At historic Appleby, the railway speciality was milk. Express Dairy was established here in 1931. A locomotive—usually an ex-Midland 4-4-0—was attached to special milk tanker-wagons, each capable of holding, at first, 3,000 gallons. They were lined by glass. At first, the tankers were fixed to the 3.26 p.m. train from Appleby. As farmers became more confident about the milk scheme, and production rose, special trains were arranged. Milk drawn from Edenvale cows one day was on London doorsteps or retail shops early on the following day.

Cattle were sent away from Appleby in horse boxes, which were known as 'prize cattle wagons'. The cows were transported over a wide area. When a horse box was being used for horses—the capacity of each box was three—one end was modified to provide a simple lodging place for the attendant. He might sleep here while travelling overnight.

When a hiker's train was de-railed at Appleby, 200 people were on Horton station. They were waiting to return to Leeds. Joe Barker, of

Beecroft Farm, was contacted by one of the staff for a supply of milk for them. Joe's wife was asked to produce some good, strong coffee. 'We provided 'em with food and drink.'

## Crosby Garrett

A junior porter at Crosby Garrett in 1934 was fifteen years old and received 15 shillings per week. He became familiar with the milk trade. The Express Dairy had lately opened at Appleby and a special milk train from Hawes called at Crosby Garrett, drawing up beside one of the longest platforms on the Midland system. In those days, 17-gallon kits were the rule. 'They weighed a fair bit when you got about ten on a barrel.' Farmers arrived with milk at the station. One or two farmers had 'cars and trailers; mostly the farmers were using horses, traps, or bits of carts'.

## Long Marton, Newbiggin, and Culgaith

The Long Marton viaduct crosses Troutbeck with a length of rather more than 100 yards. Composed of five lofty spars, it had red sandstone for its construction, this material coming from a quarry in Dufton Gill, which lies 2 miles away. Abutments, piers, and parapets were fashioned of stone. The station was closed in 1970. Newbiggin and Culgaith played a prominent part in Eden Valley events. Culgaith became an unstaffed halt in 1967, and was closed to passengers three years later. The tunnel remains open to traffic, of course. With a length of 661 yards, one can see through to the end.

## Lazonby, Armathwaite, and Scotby

Lazonby was one of the busiest of the Edenvale stations. Billy Oliphant dealt in potatoes. Vanloads of empty sacks were received and were distributed among farmers. Lazonby had the distinction of being able to grow bigger carrots than any other place along the Settle–Carlisle line; the main factor in this was the extremely sandy nature of the soil. Close to the station was a sandstone quarry, from which extracted sand was once used in the sand boxes of locomotives. Lazonby goods yard used to handle a good deal of locally-felled timber. In the autumn, the goods aspect of its life involved large numbers of sheep. Armathwaite station was built a little distance from the village. Scotby, which closed in 1942, was the most

1. Dent Station House.

2. Settle residents leaving by train for army service in the First World War.

3. A typical signal box interior.

4. A drawing of a steam train by Peter Fox.

5. Railway sleepers used to create snow fencing at Dent.

6. A drawing of a locomotive with a snow-plough attachment.

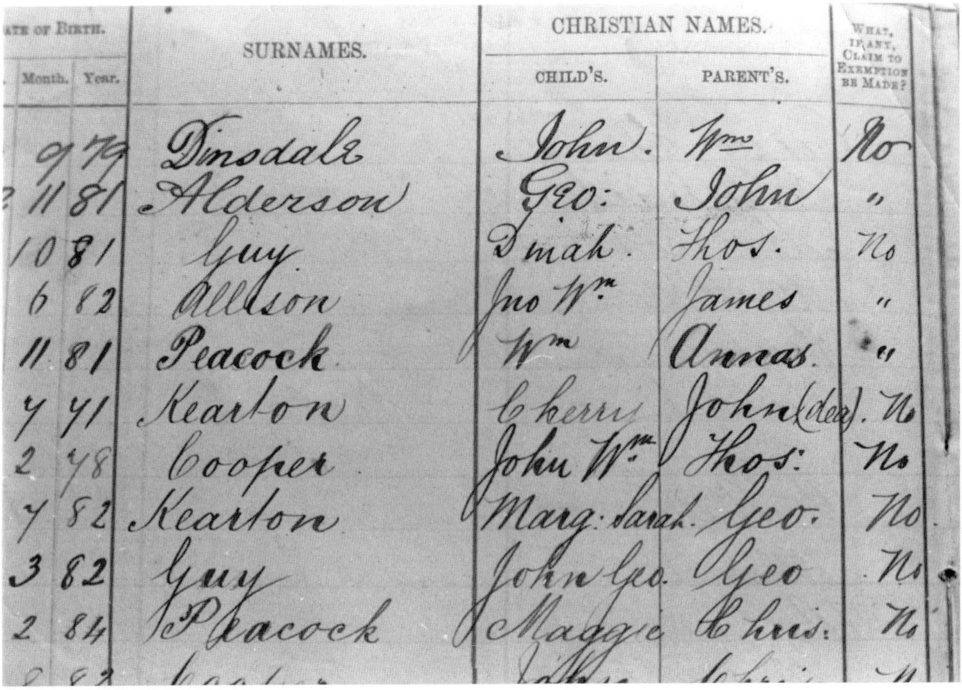

| ATE OF BIRTH. | | SURNAMES. | CHRISTIAN NAMES. | | WHAT, IF ANY, CLAIM TO EXEMPTION BE MADE? |
|---|---|---|---|---|---|
| Month. | Year. | | CHILD'S. | PARENT'S. | |
| 9 | 79 | Dinsdale | John. | Wm | No |
| 11 | 81 | Alderson | Geo: | John | " |
| 10 | 81 | Guy | Dinah. | Thos. | No |
| 6 | 82 | Allison | Jno Wm | James | " |
| 11 | 81 | Peacock | Wm | Annas. | " |
| 7 | 41 | Kearton | Cherry | John (dec). | No |
| 2 | 78 | Cooper | John Wm | Thos: | No |
| 7 | 82 | Kearton | Marg: Sarah | Geo. | No |
| 3 | 82 | Guy | John Geo. | Geo | No |
| 2 | 84 | Peacock | Maggie | Chris: | No |

7. The burial register at Chapel-le-Dale church.

8. The author on the scaffolding during the restoration of Ribblehead Viaduct.

9. Chapel-le-Dale church, the burial place of navvies.

10. A resident hangs out washing at Garsdale.

11. A steam special.

12. A steam special stops at Garsdale.

13. Memorial at Ribblehead Viaduct commemorating the restoration of the line in 1991.

14. Appleby station.

*Above:* 15. Garsdale Signal Box.

*Below:* 16. A greenhouse made from the remains of a signal box in Eden Valley.

*Above:* 17. A steam train leaves Dent station.

*Below:* 18. The redundant Settle Signal Box—now a visitors centre.

19. Salt Lake Cottages.

20. A floral display at Settle Station.

21. A steam train heading south at Garsdale.

22. A double-header at the water tank at Appleby.

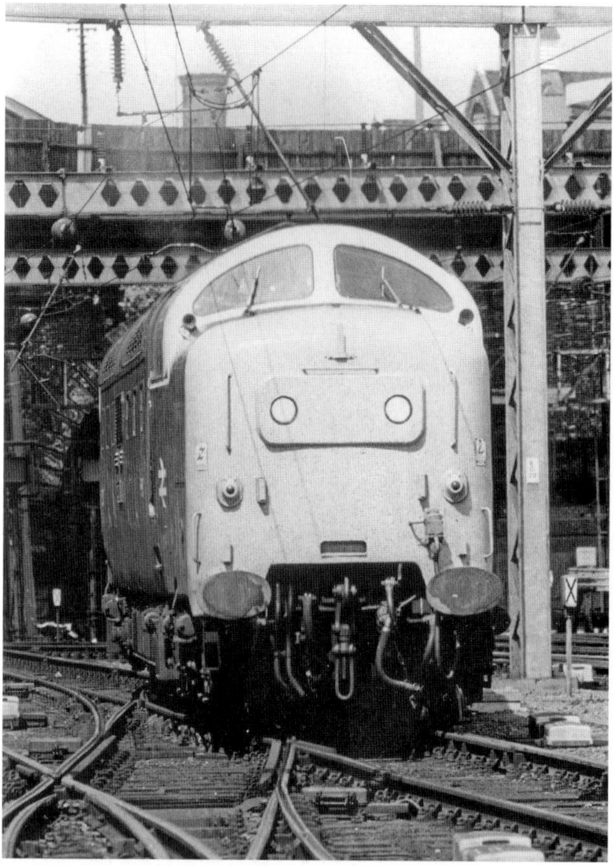

23. A diesel train leaving Carlisle.

24. Ais Gill Signal Box, at the highest point of the line..

25. Jimmy Fishwick, an ex-locomotive driver.

26. Bill Sharpe and his son—the last uniformed staff at Ribblehead.

27. The Ribblehead viaduct in winter.

28. Railway cottages in Settle.

29. A cutter on the Settle-Carlisle line during the big snow of 1947.

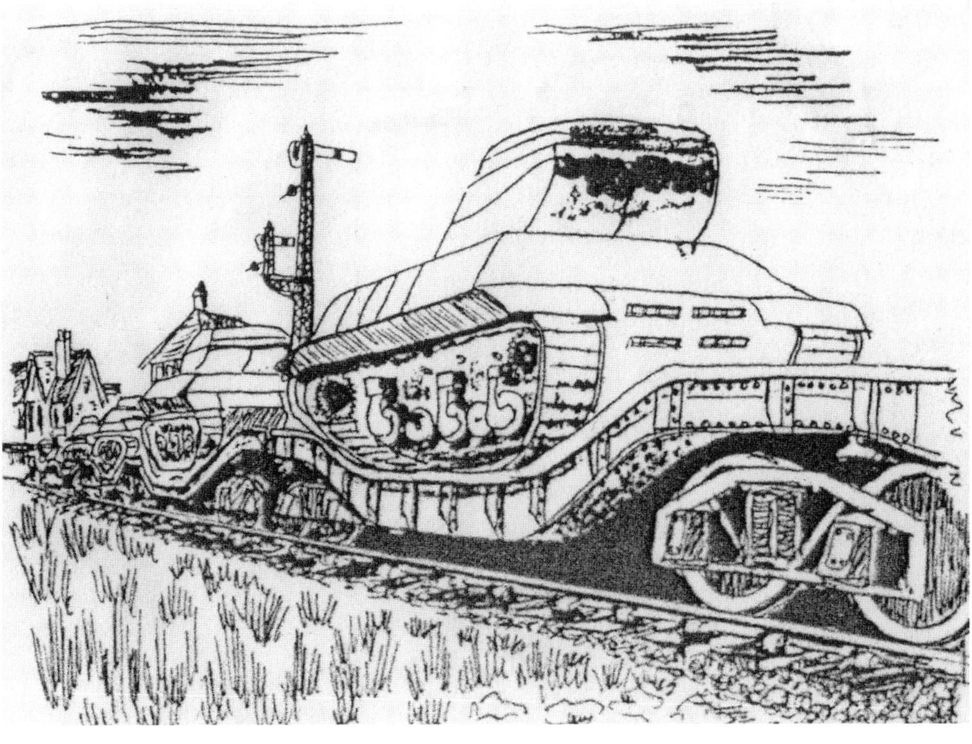

30. A wartime impression of a goods train bearing tanks without gun barrels.

31. The author (*left*) officially unveils the plaque to mark the restoration of Hellifield Station.

32. Dave Goulder (*right*), composer of Settle-Carlisle folk songs, with Tim Parker, former Station Master at Settle Station.

northerly of the Midland type. Years ago, a stationmaster at Armathwaite 'was always nattering about wanting promotion'. This was granted in a way he did not like. He left 'lovely Armathwaite' for a place 'right among the Collieries'.

## Carlisle Citadel

The 150th anniversary of the opening of Citadel Station in 1997 was celebrated with enjoyable events. Barracks for overnight accommodation were at Upperby, which stood in a loco yard. They were invariably so crowded that a man requiring a bed had to wait until one was vacated!

Of the many viaducts on the Settle–Carlisle line it is Ribblehead that continually comes into my mind. Bill Sharpe, a former stationmaster, recalled when a banking engine was summoned to the rear of a goods train in order to push it through some turbulent air. A high wind, entering the partly open sides of cattle wagons, acted as a brake, bringing the train to a halt.

One of the silliest stories told about Ribblehead related to a railwayman, who was crossing the viaduct when the wind plucked his hat from his head, passed it under an arch, and blew it back on his head from the opposite direction. I have, with official permission, walked across the viaduct on a windy day—and discovered that the parapets offered a wind-shield. A strong wind blew over my head. There was a time when, with maintenance work on the track in progress elsewhere, the viaduct was opened up to organised groups of pedestrians—over 2,000 in all. Jon Mitchell, a long-serving ITV weatherman, stood beside Mike Harding, who held the scissors that snipped the tape at the opening ceremony.

8

# Home Life: Railmen Take it Easy

A writer in *Wildman's Household Almanack* in 1875 mentioned that at Settle a row of six cottages for railway families was under construction. He wrote they were:

> ...a pretty order of architecture ... The erection of such structures shows a wise policy, as unless the men are comfortably housed it will be a difficult task to keep them at their various posts, in the solitary and dreary places through which the line passes.

Settle was neither solitary nor dreary. The design of terraced housing for railwaymen and their families usually included porches at the front. Each porch had a central partition, which gave access to adjacent cottages. At the back of many terraced dwellings was a small yard, with a washhouse and toilet. In some cases these facilities were set in a single large yard.

Salt Lake Cottages, on land adjacent to the railway, to the south of Ribblehead, were built for 'railway servants' but privatised. The name probably became familiar during missionary work by Mormons from Salt Lake City, Utah. They were known to be seeking converts in the Dales in the 1860s. The row of dwellings was typical of those erected by the Midland to house railway servants. Three double-sided projecting porches gave Salt Lake a touch of distinction.

Lily Towler took up residence at No. 3 Salt Lake on her marriage in 1932. A rent of 5 *s* per week was deducted from the wage of her husband. Before the First World War, it had cost a railwayman 2 *s* 6 *d* per week to lodge with an old ganger at Garsdale. The ganger's wife would bite the half-crown he handed to her, checking that it was real. I was told:

> ...our lodgings in one of the railway cottages had three bedrooms. There were six of us—two to a room. I often wondered where the ganger and his wife slept for the night. We found out on a night when, missing the last train from Hawes, we walked back to our lodgings. We got to the house in the early hours—just as the old lady was coming out of her dormitory—a cupboard under the stairs. The ganger also slept there!

In summertime, before the outbreak of the First World War, large numbers of Irishmen travelled to the Pennine Dales to help with the hay harvest. Many of the men were from County Mayo. They disembarked at Liverpool or Heysham and might do some work on the low-lying farms of the Fylde before moving up to the hills. The hirings they attended, usually by rail, were at Bentham, Skipton, or Hawes. On the day prior to the Hawes Hiring, a train from Garsdale to Hawes was packed with Irishmen, many of whom spent the night in local barns so that they would be available, bright and early, when the Hirings began in the main street of the town. After a month of haymaking they moved eastwards to help with the harvest at arable farms.

In the 1920s, finding employment of any kind was especially hard. An Edenvale man who applied for work on the Settle–Carlisle found that no jobs were available. He worked on a farm. His railway career began in 1923, when he went to Grassington and for three years served on the railway that ran updale from Skipton:

> I became a senior at 25 *s* a week. When I applied to get on Carlisle Citadel, I was sent to Ribblehead instead, for £2 a week. Then I came down to Armathwaite, classed as a grade-2 porter. It was 1929 and I was still getting £2 a week.

Just before the Second World War, a North Ribblesdale signalman paid 5 *s* 4 *d* to rent one of the Salt Lake Cottages. There was no running water. The residents used a tap at the end of the row, water being drawn from a tank set up in a field situated across the line. The aforementioned signalman preferred to go to a local spring for water, boiling every drop intended for human consumption. The Dawson family, who lived hereabouts for many years, shopped once a month—'We only had basic things.'

A lady who had married a signalman in 1927 told me that the signal box stood in Yorkshire but her home, 200 yards away, was in Westmorland. The railway cottage had no sink or tap. Rainwater barrels caught a share of the Pennine rainfall for the wash-house, which stood across the yard. 'It was life in the wilds. I had to pay a penny a year to the landowner for every stoop I put in to support my washing line.'

At Long Marton, I heard the following from a railway family:

> ...we used to grow just about everything we ate. The washing line was hung on the embankment, which we called The Batters. On baking day, you baked the sort of thing that would keep well in your husband's bait tin. It would be something filling and substantial. Fruit loaves, squares, rock buns. There'd be something special—a little bacon and an egg pie, in a saucer, that would do him twice. I used to cut it in two and pack one up for the day.

Before the Second World War, a platelayer received 39 *s* per week. An Appleby man who began work on the railway in 1937 sadly recalled a custom of laying off men just before their year was up, and then re-hiring them; 'If they made you "permanent" they had to give you holidays.' A member of the Davison family, who formerly worked in the tunnel maintenance gang in the Hungry Thirties, was provided with a cottage at Blea Moor.

At that time, having a regular job and somewhere to live—even if the cottage stood in the wilds, with its back to a tract of moorland—was comforting for a housewife who had been brought up on a farm in remote Grisedale. In winter she put to good use the skills she had been taught as a girl—knitting, sewing, embroidery, and the making of mats and quilts. A platelayer who had one of the Blea Moor cottages from 1955 until 1961 shopped in Settle on a Saturday. He strode to Ribblehead station. At Settle, the goods he ordered from T. D. Smith's 'came up by goods train'.

The Dawson family had a long tenure of a cottage at Blea Moor. Their home stood a good walking distance north of Ribblehead. Nancy, one of the family, recalls:

> We had one living room, a front room we never used—we just kept it for best—and three bedrooms upstairs. The house was heated by a single coal fire in the kitchen. Coal was delivered by railway, the allotted heap being dumped at the line-side. It was then moved into the wash-house. The water supply was piped from the river.

Toilet facilities were primitive—just a big hole in the ground, with a seat over the top, situated at one end of the wash-house:

> At night-time, if it was dark, we went in two's and three's with a candle, covered by a can to stop it blowing out. On windy days we could not

> dispose of the toilet paper down the hole. It just blew back. Eventually, the earth closet was replaced by a chemical toilet. John Dawson, my father, used to say, 'Them 'at uses it can empty it.' He would disappear up the fell—to a pothole!

During the wintry spell early in 1947, the Dawsons were in a white desert and Nancy was not able to attend school for twelve weeks:

> Visually, it was a spectacular winter. It snowed all night and froze all day, so the snow got deeper and firmer. You were just walking on top of the latest snowfall. Every morning we had to dig out from the back door so that we could get outdoors and get water. We had a good supply of food. Groceries were delivered.

The most dramatic moment in Nancy's life at Blea Moor was when, aged fourteen, she was sunbathing on the roof of the pig-sty when the Thames-Clyde express was derailed—a few hundred yards away from where she was reclining. It was Easter, 21 April 1952. Nancy heard a scraping sound and the noise of gushing steam; 'When I sat up, all I could see was steam. Then I saw a locomotive on its side and the first three coaches lying at strange angles.'

The up-express, a ten-coach train, had left Glasgow at 9.15 a.m.; it was a class 7P 4-6-0 Number 46117 *Welsh Guardsman*, piloted by a class-4 ex-Midland Compound No. 41040. As events turned out, it was fortunate that the coaches had steel under-frames. The train had travelled through Blea Moor tunnel at a speed of 45 mph. Members of the permanent way gang in the tunnel noticed that 'something' on the leading engine was striking the ballast. They were powerless to call attention to this. The brake rod on the Compound had loosened at one end, causing it to rotate.

The *Welsh Guardsman* fell on its near side and the first four coaches were thrown off their bogies, blocking all lines. The following four coaches, though derailed, remained upright. The last two stayed on the track. Nancy made for the scene of the accident. She found a carry-cot containing a baby—who, happily, was unharmed. The mother scrambled out of one of the side windows of a carriage and was reunited with her child. 'People started coming out of the coaches. No one seemed to be badly hurt, though there were injuries caused by flying glass.'

It was some time before the rescue party arrived. The ambulance men had a shock on reaching the scene; it was a hot day at Easter, and passengers who were not injured lay flat, sunbathing, their inert forms giving the impression to the new arrivals that they were dead. Nancy received a letter of congratulation from the Girl Guides' Association and a watch from the railway authority. Three railway cranes were at the site by 5.30 p.m., single-line working was introduced at 9.12 a.m. the next day, and by 4.40 p.m. normal service on the Settle–Carlisle was resumed.

Nancy's father worked on a stretch of the Settle–Carlisle that extended from a central position in Blea Moor tunnel, at a depth of 500 feet, to Ribblehead viaduct, which rises majestically to a height of 100 feet. Nancy said:

> I always remember my father, especially when a chimney needed sweeping. We didn't have chimney sweeps. If the fire started smoking back, he'd say, 'It's time the chimney was swept.' We all stood back when he put a detonator on the fire!

His eldest daughter was living with the family at Blea Moor when her marriage was arranged. The ceremony took place in Chapel-le-Dale church. Nancy remarked:

> You couldn't get ready for a wedding at Blea Moor. With her hair in curlers and her wedding dress resting over an arm, she got a lift on a locomotive down to Ribblehead, preparing her attire for the wedding at the Station Inn before travelling to the church.

When Margaret, a younger daughter of the Dawson family, was expecting her third child, she went into labour late one evening and had to be transported somewhere for attention:

> The only thing to do was to stop the express, which duly happened. Margaret left home with her suitcase. She was lifted on to the train, taken to Settle station—then transported to Cawder Gill Maternity hospital in Skipton, where she gave birth to a son.

Train travel could be handy. When Nancy's sister was married, she moved to a home in the vicinity of the Tyne:

> At holiday times we used to go and stay with her. On the way back, we changed at Carlisle. If we were lucky while standing on the Carlisle platform we'd meet one of an engine crew who would say, 'You must be one of Jack Dawson's lassies. We'll stop the train at Blea Moor if you like…'

The train did indeed stop, saving the young ladies a long walk from Ribblehead station.

Lodging was a familiar experience for the footplate men. The barracks at Upperby, in Carlisle, were so crowded a man had to wait a while for a bed to be vacated:

> The place was really noisy. If you have a barracks in a loco yard and there are locomotives belching smoke and steam for 24 hours a day, it's not easy to go to sleep. I don't think men would put up with it these days.

At Kingsmoor, the barracks were alongside the area where coal was tipped into the engines. 'The noise was appalling. There were never quite enough beds. As a man got out of one bed, I got in. It was still quite warm!'

In 1926 there was a General Strike in support of coal miners:

> We all received strike pay. When the strike was called off, out-of-work payments were made only if you have twelve months' membership in the union. I never heard of anyone —man or boy—being paid off between Carlisle and Dent. I was a junior and a member of the union. The porter at Appleby—possibly a junior also—was offered a transfer but was retained at Appleby as being the sole support of his mother.

The industrial slump came. During the late 1920s and until 1938, money was scarce and hard-won. Productivity, if it existed, must have been low, judging by the long intervals between freight trains on the Settle–Carlisle line.

9

# Special Deliveries: Sheep and Cattle, Coal and Limestone

With the opening of the Settle–Carlisle, supplies of coal could be transported to Settle economically. This greatly benefited John Delaney, an Irishman born in 1846. During the Hungry Forties, John's eldest sister, Anne, settled the family in Cheshire. He eventually found employment in a mill at Settle and was to cherish memories of the 1870s, when the railway came into being. Purchasing a horse and cart with £40 advanced by a Quaker banker in Sheffield, John Delaney went into a coal business. University studies having given Delaney an insight into the nature of limestone, he exploited the limestone of the Craven district by opening up quarries and transporting lime by rail to Sheffield, which was then thought of as the Steel City. Delaney's outlook on life was transformed in 1896 when he became a devout Quaker. Henceforth, his religious convictions were evident in all he said and did.

I heard from contemporaries that Delaney was of medium, broad build, with a white beard and a conspicuous nose, down which he tended to talk. He usually arrived at his Horton-in-Ribblesdale quarry in an old, chauffeur-driven Renault, one of the first cars in the district. Quarrying at that time was almost entirely handwork. A veteran quarry worker I met at Beecroft Quarry, Horton, in 1953 had started work as a labourer in 1900. He earned 4½ pence per hour. Drills used to pierce the rock to hold the explosives were hand-operated; they penetrated the quarry face for about 26 feet. The railway was a handy form of transport.

Delaney became fascinated by the railway. He had a new house called 'Overdale' built at Settle. It overlooked the railway and he was able to time rail traffic—both crack expresses and slow stopping trains. If, in bad weather, the Scottish express was late, he would rouse the household as early as 4 a.m. Another of Delaney's whims was to have water for Overdale drawn from a spring at the Horton quarry, and daily transported to Settle by rail. He preferred this water to that which came through the town's taps.

Delaney died in 1921 from the sudden onset of pernicious anaemia, for which there was no known medical cure. The lad from poverty-stricken Ireland, who made a fortune in fifteen years of lively business activity, breathed his last in his mid-seventies. There was a Quaker touch in his will—each of his workers received the sum of £5.

The Settle–Carlisle line was at the edge of a huge belt of outcropping limestone. At Willy Wood, north of Langcliffe, the Craven Lime Company erected a kiln with a chimney rather more than 200 ft in height which could be kept burning continuously. The structure contained, according to the contractor (one George Dawson of Leeds), around 200,000 bricks. This Hoffman Kiln was so designed that there could be the continuous burning of lime. Sidings connected the kiln with the Settle–Carlisle. Limestone was a major product of North Ribblesdale. At Horton, when the trade was in its heyday in the 1950s, the railway dealt with a 250,000 tons a year. Much coal was needed to fire the kilns.

*Old Limey* was a name bestowed on a regular freight train that delivered limestone to Scotland. The name was given by quarrymen working at Horton-in-Ribblesdale. 'In its heyday we were preparing three fully-loaded, northward-bound trains per day.' *Old Limey* left Hellifield at about 2.40 p.m. with Carlisle men on the footplate. Limestone quarried on the top of Moughton Fell was brought down by an incline railway working on the principle that laden trucks descending would draw up a line of empties. The old quarrymen who had to work on Good Friday called it Runaway Friday. If anything was going to break loose, it would occur then.

As already noted, banking empty wagons at Horton could be spectacular. A former stationmaster at Horton-in-Ribblesdale remarked:

> You might bank about forty to fifty empty wagons up. You had to give 'em full throttle. The train was drawn out of the station to beyond the starting signal. Then the signalman had to turn the points for going inside, round the corner to Settle Limes quarry. There were two road ups—a front road and a back road. The empties went up the front road so we had to be absolutely sure that particular set of points was right (if you'd gone in the back road, you'd have been in terrible trouble). Towards the end of the front road, instead of running on to the stop blocks, there was another set of points that diverted you round the corner.

So everything was set.

> The driver took the train right out of the station, up the line. If he had a lot on, he'd go further than usual. If he hadn't got so many on, he needn't go so far. When we knew the road was clear, our shunter would be given the tip. He'd give the tip to me. I was down at the front road. I'd give the tip to the driver to come on. As soon as he'd got that, he opened the regulator full and—WHAM; clank, clank, clank, clank, clank! zzzzz! He used to go round the corner—and perhaps he'd stick. He wouldn't get them all round. Derailments were not uncommon. We had a favourite set of points where there were more derailments than I'd ever known. We got wagons back on the track with ramps— or using the Hellifield steam crane. We didn't often need this, thank goodness.

The Foredale quarry at Helwith Bridge was known as Nibble. There was only rail access. Every evening, chippings from Foredale were conveyed by rail to the Craven Quarry near Langcliffe.

The Settle–Carlisle had a farming flavour. From Leeds to Carlisle there were part-time cattle drovers. The signal box in Hunslet Lane in Leeds was opened so that cattle due to arrive from Heysham and Scotland could—after so many hours of travel—be watered. Two or three members of Gang 201, who worked on the south-eastern side of Appleby, had a pleasant and lucrative sideline at haytime. They had business connections with a farmer and dropped off the ballast train at a point from which they were almost immediately in the hayfield—and in cash. They might also snatch some light refreshments. Gang 18, working at Hawes in haytime, joined some July Barbers, the nickname for Irish haytime workers. When ponies were working down the mines, a goodly number were purchased at Brough Hill horse fair, held near Warcop. Horses and ponies were entrained at Kirkby Stephen Midland station. A large number had not been broken in and, alas, the bewildered animals were beaten with a stick. At Settle, where the cattle dock consisted of a dozen pens, railwaymen handled goats and tups, ducks and day-old chicks, and also hens in crates. Occasionally, a wagon containing cattle from Ireland would arrive to be collected by a cattle dealer. Tups being brought back to Dent from the sales at Kirkby Stephen were quartered in the guard's van.

Tuesday, market day at Settle, brought an influx of rural folk to the town by rail. In the crowd were women with baskets containing locally produced pats of butter, cheese and eggs. Bell Pratt, a cattle dealer who had business connections in the Highlands and Islands of Scotland, used the station at Garsdale for his travels and as a temporary depot for his Scottish purchases. These dark and stocky animals were summered, then sold. Settle station yard was periodically invaded by farm animals. A special task was receiving horses that had been consigned by rail to the Dawsons of Langcliffe Hall. The horses, sent up in summer, were kept into the autumn, when they were used as mounts by the grouse-shooters.

From Leeds to Carlisle there were part-time cattle drovers. A signal box in Hunslet Lane was opened so that Irish cattle arriving via Heysham and from Scotland could be watered. This had to be done after a specified number of hours. The Ribblehead sheep sales, held adjacent to the railway station, had a gala atmosphere. Turners, the auctioneers, arranged for pens to be placed beside the station approach. Dent had a cattle dock that lost its importance when motor wagons became common. In the 1930s, it was not unusual, at a rural station, to see calves reclining in hessian sacks; the calves were being sent to Leeds by passenger train. Tups, being brought back to Dent from the sales at Kirkby Stephen, were quartered in the guard's van.

In the heyday of the cattle trade at Hellifield, stock from Heysham Docks arrived at about 4 a.m. The men at Heysham had packed the cows like sardines:

> They had usually been on the rails for so long they had to be taken from the wagons to be watered. This meant their size expanded. There was always 'one over' and it had to go in another wagon.

Hellifield also received, by van, cows from Scotland. They arrived in the early hours and were usually sold during the same day. 'Whoever bought 'em might want 'em to go by rail. So it was a matter of—back to the station with them!' The movement of livestock was considerable, especially at Lazonby, where around 800 railway wagon loads per year were of farm stock.

The cattle dock at Settle consisted of a dozen pens. Occasionally, a wagon of Irish cattle would arrive for a cattle dealer. They were taken away by Old Mick, commonly known as the Bull Walloper. He delivered them to an area at the rear of the Royal Oak Hotel, where they were put up for sale. At the end of the day, Mick was supposed to return unsold beasts to the railway station so they might be sold elsewhere.

An astonishing number of tups, purchased at Kirkby Stephen or Hawes, were railborne to the district where their new homes were sited. Sheep farmers living at Keasden, on the moors opposite the village of Clapham, travelled to a market by train, via Settle. Later that day they might be seen returning with the animals they had bought. Disembarking from a train at Settle, they walked their tups to Giggleswick railway station to catch a train to Clapham, from where the now-weary tups were led on a steeply-rising road to their new homes.

Every October, until shortly after the Second World War, a vast number of cattle trucks were marshalled at sidings connected with the two stations at Kirkby Stephen. This was in readiness for the cattle and sheep sales at what was grandly known as Luke Fair. Cattle were housed in pens set up in the Market Square. Sheep were held in pens erected on both sides of Market Street, into the quaintly-named Sow Pow and down Melbreaks. Droves of cattle were then driven to one or other of the local railway stations. Men who volunteered as drovers—and were paid for their pains—were especially keen to drive cattle to the station on the Settle–Carlisle line. It was the greatest distance of the two stations; the pay was better!

Things did not always go according to plan. When Leonard Bousfield (who lived at Gordon House, in the centre of Kirkby Stephen) took a drove up the main street, heading for the Midland station, a house was defiled by an incontinent cow. This coincided with the lady owner's doorstep scrubbing. She had temporarily left the front door of the house open. A cow entered, walked down the passage, turned into the kitchen—and deposited a heap of quaking dung. The man usually stuttered. What he said to the lady owner might be translated as: 'Be quick. Get it cleaned up—otherwise it'll set like cement.'

Motor cattle wagons became common after the Second World War. Each autumn, a special sheep train, hired by Craven flockmasters, ran from Bell Busk to the Eden Valley, where sheep were wintered in the root-fields. Another train brought them back to their home farms for lambing. At Lazonby, when Johnny Graham, a most colourful character, was in charge of the so-called cattle dock, he supervised the unloading of sheep that had been purchased in Scotland one Monday. On the following Wednesday, sixty-five wagons were expected.

Lazonby also had a lively trade in rabbits. Three local dealers took them around the county villages twice or three times a week. Rabbits were crated and despatched from Lazonby station to Bradford or Leeds. Some were transported to Newcastle. During the Second World War, a crate containing twenty couples of rabbits was despatched by train at a cost of 6 *s* 3 *d*. One lady managed to get thirty rabbits in a crate—plus a couple of pheasants 'tucked in between where you couldn't see 'em'. Lazonby also saw pigeons entrained for distant parts, from where they were released to fly back to their lofts.

Appleby was one of the first places from which prize cattle were sent away in boxes. The so-called 'prize cattle wagons' were really horse-boxes—smart affairs, each holding three horses, with a seat at one end for the attendant. Also to be seen at Appleby were geese in sacks, the birds being sent off for breeding. Just after the Second World War, racehorses were transported from Northallerton to Garsdale, from where—via the Settle–Carlisle—they were destined to take part in races at Carlisle or Ayr. The return journey took place the following day. Anhydrite workings were opened south of Cumwhinton. Long Meg gave her name to a gypsum mine, the rock being transported by rail to Widnes. Railway sidings were installed at Long Meg. During the course of the next two decades, about 2,000,000 tons of 'blue cobble' passed over the Settle–Carlisle.

Gypsum from Drax power station is transported to the plaster board factory at Kirkby Thore in the Eden Valley. There is an almost daily timber train, its wagons holding neat stacks of freshly-felled young conifers from the upper dales.

10

# Accidents: Trains off The Line

Accidents have been few—but spectacular. In September 1913, a sleeper train from Glasgow to St Pancras halted half a mile north of Ais Gill, summit of the Settle–Carlisle.

The engine had run short of steam. The quality of the coal was poor. The driver had no pilot to assist him. The sleeper was being followed by a night train from Inverness and Edinburgh. The crew were having difficulties on the footplate because of poor quality coal. Being preoccupied with trying to get sufficient steam, they over-ran the signals at Mallerstang and collided with the back of the stationary train. Fire broke out and fourteen people were killed.

The most serious accident occurred in 1960—a time when steam trains were operating and anyone waking up during the night would, sooner or later, hear a train making noisy progress up the Drag. I recall waking up at my home, which is within sight of the line. It was January 11 and there was a protracted period of silence; I wondered if the line had been blocked by an overnight blizzard. On the edge of town, a major incident involving two locomotives—a passenger and a goods train—were being attended by railwaymen, firemen, and ambulance men. Arc lamps had been brought to the big embankment leading to Langcliffe. A steam crane was there, helping to disentangle and remove the wreckage.

Gradually, the story could be pieced together. The driver of a Britannia-class locomotive working the Glasgow to St Pancras night express had stopped at Garsdale to examine his engine, but did not notice that both the right-hand side-bars had dropped off. At Settle, the connecting rod fell away from the piston and ploughed into the track. A 'down' goods train was detailed and struck the St Pancras train, causing the death of five passengers.

Reference has been made to the Easter holiday of 1952, when Nancy Dawson, then a fourteen-year-old schoolgirl, was living with her family at a Blea Moor cottage, close to the railway; she decided to sunbathe on the flat roof of the pig-sty, which stood in a corner of the garden. It was, indeed, only 100 yards or so from where an express train left the rails. The accident could have been a lot worse than it turned out to be:

> My mother was there. My father was at work. There was a handy signalman. The first thing I found was a baby in a carry-cot; they had come through one of the carriage windows. The baby's mother emerged from one of the side windows and was re-united with the child. The injuries were not very bad, being mostly cuts from broken glass. One boy had been thrown through a window and had quite bad lacerations and damaged legs. We took him into the house and put him on the sofa in the front room. We bandaged his legs.

The first reaction of Nancy's mother when the smash occurred was to put the kettle on so there might be lots of cups of tea for the passengers when they went into the house:

> It was a long time before anyone came to attend to the accident. They parked at Winterscales and walked up from there. It was a beautiful sunny day. When they arrived, everyone else was lying on a bank. They were sun-bathing. The ambulance and rescue services thought they were dead.

11

# Wild Weather: Rain, Wind, Fog, Snow

A driver arriving at Ribblehead was asked by the Stationmaster to put some more coal on the locomotive fire. He wanted to see which way the wind was blowing! On the Settle–Carlisle, the elements tested the wits and stamina of the footplate men. Tinted leaves falling in autumn might inspire a poet. In a wet state, settling on the tracks on a shadowy stretch such as Stainforth Cutting, many a proud train came to a standstill, though its wheels continued to spin. In wild weather, the turntable at Garsdale was a major talking point. A strong wind might blow a locomotive round and round, out of control; a barrier of sleepers was raised round the turntable to cheat the wind. At Blea Moor, 'fog men' sat in a lile cabin near the distant signal. 'When t'signal was on, he put a detonator on t'rail. When t'signal came off, he put yon detonator off. If t'distant remained on, and a train went ower it, he cracked it!'

Most memories concerned heavy snowfalls. The Great Blizzard of February 1947 found a sure place in Settle–Carlisle folklore.

A porter who lived at the Railway Cottages in Settle normally left home for work by the back door, walked along the backs of the cottages and up the railway banking. This way was blocked. He struggled along a snowy road and reached his point of work at 9.30 a.m., two hours later than usual. He found that the snow was level with the windows of railway buildings. It looked as though it had been piled up deliberately. In the yard, the wagons on the sidings were overblown. And, of course, the Settle–Carlisle line was closed.

Prisoners of war were brought up in ballast trains to clear snow out of Ribblehead Station. The snow was emptied over the parapets of the viaduct. One lot of prisoners refused to get out of a train to clear snow. When eventually the inspector got them out and the wagons had been filled, he took them to the viaduct. They would not empty the wagons. The inspector, a religious man, had been never heard to swear as much. When trains had been brought to a halt at the bridge near Salt Lake Cottages, one of the drivers shouted to a local lady, 'Would you like some black snow?' He brought her half a sack of coal. She had just had a pig killed—and exchanged it for some bacon.

Jack Towler and his men were returning from working at Blea Moor. It was 5 p.m. The weather was misty:

> We got as far as Ribblehead and heard a big aeroplane coming over. It was droning away. I says, 'He'll have to look out, the way he's going.' We didn't get much further when there was such a bang. A Lancaster bomber had crashed into Whernside.

The next morning, Jack looked through the staircase window onto the fell—and saw the remains of the huge plane. The five crew members perished. Their bodies were reverently carried to Winterscales Farm and placed in the sitting room until they were claimed by the RAF.

The line was snow-blocked for weeks, though trains continued to run from Hawes to Garsdale. Food for folk who lived beside the line was piled up on the engine. Snow ploughs were decked with fodder for starving farm animals. The RAF delivered bales of hay by air. One pilot was so precise in a hay drop that at Garsdale a bale went through a farmhouse roof. At Blea Moor, 'snow men' cleaned the points and attended any signals that were obscured by snow.

The line between Ribblehead Viaduct and Blea Moor tunnel became blocked and residents at a railway cottage received a message that they should remain indoors one day—a snow-blower was due to arrive, and snow would fly in all directions. Nancy Dawson recalls:

> Mother and I went upstairs to watch a phenomenon—the revolutionary jet engine, from a factory at Barnoldswick. It had been placed on a flat truck—and got stuck! My father remarked, 'The only thing that will shift that snow is a lot of men with shovels.' Dad sat at the lineside—and lit his pipe! The cutting was eventually dug out by prisoners of war. Men with shovels!

Harold Harper, of Garsdale, was snow-cutting at Ais Gill on a bitterly cold day when an express stopped so that its pilot engine could be disconnected. A passenger looking from a window shouted, 'My dad said that if you got on the railway you would have bread and butter for life!' A pause. He then remarked, 'You haven't got much jam on it.' One man told of the day when he found the cutting on 'the Garsdale side of Dent station' was blocked with snow. As he walked on the drifts he could touch an aqueduct that crossed high above the line. Winter conditions were cruel for men on the permanent way. A man who worked on the Garsdale troughs one Sunday in winter stood back as a train went by, picked up water and 'splashed water about'. The spray turned to ice as it hit the tracks. 'If you wanted to lose some nuts and bolts, you got a pick and chipped the ice off.'

Men who worked on the Settle–Carlisle were keen to recall, in vivid detail, the big snows of 1942, 1947, and 1963. One of the railwaymen found himself walking up the roof of the waiting room at Dent station. In the early 1940s, Old Charlie, a ganger who lived at Dent, went to the front door one morning and couldn't see out because of drifts of snow. He went to the back door and there was snow piled up everywhere. To get out, he picked up the shovel he always kept in the house in winter-time. He asked his wife to empty the larder, which she did. He filled up the larder with snow—and got into the back yard. He had managed to get to work.

As mentioned earlier, Dent, high and prone to snowdrifts, was fitted with snow fences —several lines of railway sleepers set on a side of the cutting and on part of the moor. Dent also had cabins, where men engaged in snow-cutting and ploughing could rest up and have a meal of sorts. The cabins were declared to be 'rough' but welcome. 'Any port in a storm!' You were up there to do a job, not sit in a cabin. In and around Dent, the railway was impassable for eight weeks. A Hellifield man who often drove snow-ploughs charged a drift at Dent:

> We got into the drift—and came to a dead stand. So I got out of the cab and went to my colleague at the front engine. As I passed the engine, I walked up a heap of snow. Well below my feet was the chimney of the loco. We had to dig ourselves out.

An Edenvale man, a member of a maintenance gang, left home one Friday night following a snowstorm. His family did not see him again until the following Wednesday. He was stranded—and returned home via Newcastle! At Kirkby Stephen, conditions were so bad that men who were snow-cutting were seen to hang their coats on the tops of telegraph poles! Salt Lake Cottages, near Ribblehead, were cut off by drifts. The Thoresbys and other local families could not get their children to school for six weeks. The railway company thoughtfully provided a light engine and brake for the conveyance of groceries to families living at the lineside. The football crew also gave them some of the coal from the tender!

In 1926, a Leeds crew was the first to open up 'across the top' after a period of snow blockage. The Ais Gill signal box was submerged by snow, the only visible objects being the cross-trees of the telephone wires. The signalman had scrambled out of his box through a window. In the early 1930s, the Settle–Carlisle had been issued with all-steel snow ploughs, a type that fitted on the front buffer beam. They succeeded large wooden ploughs. During March 1933, several men were told to dig out the cutting at Ais Gill. They were directed to the starter signal. 'A few feet of t'pinnacle were sticking out of snow. You couldn't see the arm. Every cutting was full. We had twenty-five ballast wagons. We filled every one of them with snow.'

A snow plough of the 1940s consisted of two locomotives of the 0-6-0 type. There was a plough at either end so you might plough in reverse. Tarpaulin sheets covered the exposed part of the cab, which might also have the protection of side-blinds. A snow plough delivered oil, and also edibles—meat and bread—to folk who had been cut off by large snowdrifts. Accommodation vans were provided for teams of men. At Mallerstang, when snow lay at depths of 15 to 20 feet, I was told that 'there hadn't been much snow. It was the wind that did the damage.'

In 1942, Polish troops were sent to help with snow-clearing. Driven to Garsdale, and having no wellingtons to wear, they refused to leave the train. In 1947, troops who had mustered at Hadrian's Camp, Carlisle, had only mess tins and small entrenching shovels. In charge of this party were an officer and several NCOs. They lined the men up on a platform at Carlisle and found food for them.

During the 1947 blockage a pioneering jet engine was obtained from Rolls Royce at Barnoldswick and placed on a flat wagon, set to work snow-clearing on the southern side of Blea Moor. The snow was hard-packed; the experiment ended when a mere 30 yards of snow had been cleared. The engine would probably have been effective if the snow had fallen recently.

Snow-clearers developed keen appetites. Men working at Horton-in-Ribblesdale ordered food from Mr Mackintosh of the Wenhaven Bakery at Settle. Their request was for 200 soups and 200 packets of sandwiches for chaps clearing the line. The food was collected by men who went down to Settle on the snow-plough. Dent also had foul-weather cabins built of stone, which benefited crew members who were changing over. The cabins had a special role at snow-time, providing cover for men who had been mustered to clear snow drifts. Each cabin had a huge central fireplace with a firespot at each end, and there were tables—but no bunks! 'You bunked down wherever you could.'

In 1963, when snow began to fall in around mid-February, two trains were buried. A train caught on the line flanking Mallerstang was lost to sight. Another was buried in Shale Cutting, south of Dent. A local railman told me, 'It was completely buried; you couldn't see anything.' That winter, troops were summoned as needed. One hundred and fifty men had a battle with nature. Isaac Hailwood, a long-term engine driver living at Hellifield, was a regular at the photographic class I attended at Hellifield. He loved talking about cameras, but he never seemed to get round to taking photographs. One week he arrived with a camera he had just bought; he mentioned having 'shot off' a film. We took it into the dark room and developed it; the result was first-rate pictures of the cutting at Dent, with his locomotive waist-deep in snow!

Pennine gales were full of spite. A loco driver said, 'I've been on a job with a Derby 4. We stopped for water at Blea Moor. Goods trains were stopped and wagon sheets checked before they crossed Ribblehead viaduct.' At Blea Moor there was a store containing thirty or forty replacement wagon sheets. 'All t'farms round about had wagon sheets that had been wafted off trains as they crossed the viaduct on an ultra-windy day. I've seen sheets float like parachutes for about half a mile.' He looked at the moor and added, 'There'll still be a few wagon sheets out there.'

Ribblehead was noted for the changeability of the weather. Mist would blow over, dense cloud might develop, and then a railwayman might be called out for 'fogging' duties. An hour later, the sun might be shining. In the prolonged frosts of 1929, the condition of the tracks led to concern. Simon Fothergill and others were set to work at viaducts; they were 'flagging' (cautioning) to ensure that trains were not moving too fast. Simon had no hut or cabin in which to shelter; he contracted pneumonia and died. His widow continued to live at Moorcock Cottages, and she derived a small income through taking in lodgers.

Mr Harper, a Garsdale ganger, was roused by Ted Ashton, the signalman on duty at Blea Moor box. He had reported that some cars were lying in Blea Moor Tunnel. Ted stopped a train 'on the up road', which gave the ganger a lift to Blea Moor, dropping him at the north-end of the tunnel. He walked through. No cars were seen. He phoned from the end of the tunnel and the driver brought the train slowly through. He continued his walk as far as Ribblehead viaduct; about six cars lay on their bonnets on the 'up' road. It was a wild night and Ted concluded that a freak gust of wind had lifted them from their wagons. They were not normally fastened down.

12

# Wartime Memories: In Two World Wars

At the beginning of the Second World War, ninety trains passed along the Settle–Carlisle every weekday. It became a prime wartime route. Trains were sometimes 'blocked' as far back as Horton-in-Ribblesdale. A train might stand at the same place for eight hours, unable to get a down-line clearance through to Carlisle. One freight train, journeying from Hellifield to Carlisle, stood on the main line for seventeen-and-a-half hours. Wartime regulations decreed that black curtains covered the windows. A major immigration of families, trebling the population, had occurred in 'railway time'.

Even in 1939, before war had been declared, there was much military material being transported on the Settle–Carlisle line, which—happily—was in good order, much of the track having been re-laid. Sandy's wartime staff consisted of Violet Sutton and Bill Chapman, who were classified as porter-signalmen. Violet wore 'civvies'. The station was blacked out, and a hand-lamp was placed at the end of each platform to help drivers. The trains that clattered through Dent station were longer and heavier than ever. In 1942, two Jubilee locomotives that had been re-built with larger boilers made an appearance. A year later, Scots of the 4-6-0 arrangement made a local debut.

Early in the war, men who were not young or fit enough to join the armed forces might enlist in the LDV—Local Defence Volunteers, commonly referred to as Look, Duck, and Vanish! The name was changed to the Home Guard. Members sustained a guard on Ribblehead viaduct, with a single rifle and about half a dozen rounds of ammunition. The duty men used the station as their base. It was here where an exchange of the rifle, one man to another, took place. A man who presumed that cartridges were kept separately pulled the trigger of the rifle. Bang. A bullet passed through the ceiling of the waiting room and cracked some of the roof slates immediately above. A former stationmaster at Dent mentioned the movement of American servicemen and equipment that followed the USA entry into the war. An unusual sight was that of a train made up of flat trucks to which jeeps had been harnessed. Each jeep had a driver. The night was so cold the men kept the jeep engines running!

Locomotives became rough. 'Everything became rough … It was hard work on the Drag. Clonk, clonk, clonk.' The wife of a driver might not see her husband for several days at a stretch. 'I went on duty one Saturday night—and she did not see me again until the following Thursday.' The Lancaster–Carlisle line took most of the traffic. I chatted with a man who, when crossing a road bridge at Langcliffe, looked down into a cutting and saw a passing train. The roof of each carriage was boldly marked by a red cross; this was an ambulance on rails, hopefully free from enemy attacks.

A guard on a goods train that was rattling along the fell-edge track near Dent on a sunny morning—he was languidly smoking a pipe—was admiring the views. Then his attention switched to a Spitfire aircraft, which flew alongside the train for a short distance. The pilot and guard waved at each other. German aircraft were to be heard droning over the station on most nights. Flares, incendiaries, and the occasional bomb were dropped, the sound being deadened at the peaty areas. A Lancaster bomber with a Canadian crew crash-landed on the fell. The rear gunner was the only member of the crew to survive. He found his way to the Stationmaster's house, where he received medical attention from Sandy and his wife Margaret.

A lengthman told me that the war was one of the smokiest periods in the existence of Blea Moor Tunnel:

> All this wartime traffic came and filled the place with smoke; you couldn't see your hand before your face. If you got an hour, or an hour and a-half's work done during the day, it was considered to be quite good. You'd do better on a Sunday when there wasn't as much traffic.… Through the week I've seen us do practically nothing. You used to get filthy black. You had to stand so close to a wall you'd be touching it. There'd be half an inch of soot on that wall. When you came out of t'tunnel you were as black as a fire-back.

The guard of a train recalled:

> We joined the queue at Settle Junction. At Armathwaite, the signalman said we would be kept waiting for two hours. So I walked into the village

> for some sandwiches. At the pub, I was offered some—on one condition. I must make up a team for a game of dominoes. I was there at least an hour before I got my sandwiches. I was really hungry. But—just fancy—we had a game of dominoes while working between Settle and Carlisle!

A signal box incorporated an air raid shelter, the operative being provided with a tin hat. One wartime tale re-told with gusto concerned a time when some of the signal boxes were operated by women. A driver had been accustomed to entering the box, remarking to a signalman, 'Come on: get 'em off.' His reference was to the pegs that operated the signal arms; if you were on mileage work you wanted to keep the train running. A Leeds fireman entered a box on the Drag and said, 'Come on: get 'em off.' That day a signalwoman was on duty. Thinking that he meant something else, she slapped his face and said she would report him!

The Settle–Carlisle was a prime route during the Second World War. A fireman mentioned a 'funny stretch' in Lazonby Bank, where iron sleepers had been set as an experiment. It was not a success. The line carried many special trains, some with troops, and others with prisoners of war. A prisoner of war train stopped at Hellifield. Some of the American soldiers who were in charge of it were seen to be carrying Tommy-guns. Tanks were entrained to Warcop, an Army training ground. During transit by rail, the gun barrels of tanks were invariably removed.

At Grizeburn, one night, a guard visited the signal box. He was on a trainload of American soldiers. The train had been stopped seven times because soldiers were hanging their coats over the communication cord, which to them was just 'a lile bit o' red chain passing through the carriage'. The Americans were generous. At a Settle–Carlisle station, one of them tossed a 200 packet of cigarettes out of a carriage window. Other soldiers were known to throw out chewing gum, boxes of peanut butter, and packs of Chesterfield and Camel cigarettes. 'It's a wonder that no-one was killed in the rush.' Some Americans were known to fire live bullets at rabbits they saw in the fields.

An old friend of mine, who was an engine driver during the war, mentioned the blackness of night travel in the locomotive. The footplate was shielded from above. As the train headed north, there were no lights at farms and villages to give the crew a hint of where they were. 'If you couldn't see, you could at least hear and were accustomed to the distinctive sounds of viaducts, over-bridges and cuttings.'

Just before the Second Front (the invasion of Europe) took place, a trainload of jeeps were seen heading south. Americans were sitting on the jeeps, and, it being a cold time, they had kept the jeep engines running. They also kept the lights burning, which meant that when viewed from the rear the train was a blaze of red. The drivers of other trains couldn't reckon it up. The trains using the line became longer and heavier, which meant that some of the viaducts had to be strengthened. The Armathwaite viaduct was filled with concrete. Lunds viaduct was concreted between the spandrels.

Some trucks of an ammunition train broke away at Blea Moor and careered down the 1 in 100 gradient towards Settle at frightening speed. They came to rest, happily with their wheels still on the track, near Long Preston, having travelled out of control for 16 miles. A short freight train drew up for water by the 'down' platform at Appleby. The train consisted of the loco, two fitted freight wagons containing sheeted packing cases, two wagons, and a passenger coach (with no lights showing). On the bogie bolsters were what looked like two large torpedoes—miniature submarines to be used for secret attacks in Norwegian waters.

Tales of jam, whisky, and a suspected rail invasion flavoured the wartime years at Hellifield, which—as mentioned—lay outside the Settle–Carlisle line but served it. In those days, Hellifield had a refreshment room, and in a cellar-like room it kept a supply of strong drink in barrels or crates. Two Compton Mackenzie-type stories, each quite true, concern Hellifield station. In 1926, during the General Strike, there had been much talk about jam and whisky. With regard to the Strike, the staff at Hellifield station was skeletal, consisting of the stationmaster, a porter, and two ladies in the refreshment room. In the halcyon days, the caterers were a manageress, three waitresses, a cook, and a cellar man. Normally, local farmers were attracted to this facility by the quality of its ale. A railwayman arriving for a snack might bring with him a bucket of coal to augment the stock that fed a coal fire. A lad with a basket laden with fruit and chocolates greeted the passengers of each stopping train. Luncheon baskets were also available.

Only a handful of people were supposed to know that vans containing a large number of cases of jam and whisky were lodged in the railway sidings at Hellifield; there was a fear that they might be pilfered. A guard consisting of three special constables was organised by Captain Denton, then living at Riversdale, Long Preston. He asked Major J. E. E Yorke, of Halton Place, to help him. This led to raising, at short notice, a further thirty people. Major Yorke told me, 'We had shifts of six or eight men each night until 12 o'clock ... At midnight the police took over from us.' Memories of the first night were blunted when, at the changeover, Captain Denton produced a case of champagne. The volunteers were in party mood. They found their way home by various means. The special jam-and-whisky guard lasted until the end of the general strike. Nothing was stolen.

During the Second World War, the Home Guard, which evolved from the Local Defence Volunteers, was alerted about a possible invasion when a rough map was found on a bus at Burnley. It was, indeed, a map of Craven, up to Oughtershaw, with the names of several farms underlined. Each had a scribbled note, two of them being 'Irish friends here' and 'Withdraw to here', with the accompanying words 'Friends here'. Such bizarre notes implied that Hellifield station had been taken over by an Irish army commanded by a German captain! The police asked that a contingent of the Home Guard should be present to repel any invaders. They would be at the station buildings.

A contingent of the Home Guard—augmented by some 'Old Contemptibles'—would patrol the area outdoors. The password was 'Salmon'. Thirty rifles and about 200 rounds of ammunition were collected at Wakefield. The rifles were covered in grease that had been smeared on them when they had been laid up in 1918. The defenders of Hellifield were bored by the coming of dawn after having a long, eventless wait at their posts. The guard was mounted for about a month. As they said in the dale-country, 'Nowt 'appened.'

# Epilogue

Harry Speight, who penned fine books about the Yorkshire Dales, turned his attention to the Settle–Carlisle in 1892. He wrote:

> The picture of this proposed Alpine railway was a gloomy one, yet the whole of the obstacles have been overcome and the line is now rendered one of the best, safest and quickest railway routes in the kingdom. In fact, a stranger to the district might apprehend nothing remarkable during his flight between Settle and Carlisle and would hardly realise where the difficulties have been.

Frederick W. Houghton (1948) considered that 'few save railwaymen have enjoyed the privilege of, say, standing on Dent Head Viaduct to gaze down the long, green miles of verdant Dentdale'.

Steam was phased-out of the Settle–Carlisle railway in the mid-1960s. A few special, steam-hauled trains remain for excursions. When Gateshead closed, steam locomotives were moved to Leeds. Drivers and firemen who operated this line had to tackle a variety of engines. Hellifield was one of the first sheds to be closed. This took place in 'about June time'. A driver recalled that he with other drivers and firemen moved down to a base at Skipton. The shed at Hellifield was, for a time, the repose of preserved locomotives, including *Green Arrow*. Ten years after steam had been phased out, *Green Arrow* returned in typical Settle–Carlisle weather. At Ribblehead, the train was dulled by mist. Wind blew sleet across a group of railway fans who had assembled at Ribblehead to watch it go by.

Driver Cyril Patrickson took the *Flying Scotsman* over the line. The wife of one of the volunteers remarked, 'He's bin mucked-up wi' steam for years. Now he comes home from his diesel clean and tidy. I'm going to make sure he stays that way...'

Geoffrey G. Hoare, on a visit to Garsdale station, was joined by an old railwayman as he sat on a station bench, eating a sandwich lunch:

> Like most of the older staff 'up here' he preferred to live in the past. The Settle–Carlisle's glory is largely history and it is left to those of us who, as Bacon once said, 'by diligence and observation seek to recover something from the deluge of time'.

My home overlooks a tract of the Settle–Carlisle north of Settle. I am thrilled when, now and again, a steam-hauled special train goes gallantly by.

# Appendix: Songs of the Settle–Carlisle

Mr Ashwell, who had obtained Contract No. 1, also built a Mission Room at Ribblehead. Singing entered the story of the Settle–Carlisle when Mr Tiplady, a missionary, was appointed by the Midland and Bradford City Mission. Sankey-type hymns were sung at the Sunday services. On Saturday evenings, Penny Readings were popular, the programme consisting of songs of the day, interspersed with verse, some evoking laughter and others stimulating tears. Religious services were subsequently held in the waiting rooms of Ribblehead and Garsdale. At Ribblehead, the Vicar of Ingleton arrived at monthly intervals. Hymns were sung to the wheezy strains of a harmonium. Occasional dances took place in the waiting room. Music was provided by gramophone records brought by George Horner, who lived at Salt Lake Cottages.

A *Daily Express* reporter, visiting the station at Garsdale Head in the summer of 1937, attended a monthly service of the type that was a feature of local life for fifty years. The officiating clergyman, Reverend F. G. Baldrick, arrived carrying a little bag that held his miniature communion plate and vestments. The reporter found:

> ...the station platform was deserted except for the sudden roar of a train on its way to Scotland ... The dim organ music came from the waiting room. Women's voices sang a hymn.

Signalman George Gamsby had loaned the vicar a small harmonium. He and a porter carried it up to the platform and installed it at one end of the waiting room. Mrs Wilson, the wife of a railway foreman, distributed the hymn books and also laid a cloth over a small table which served as an altar. The bishop had given permission for communion to be celebrated. The worshippers 'sang with vigour'. They were standing in front of railway posters advertising holiday resorts. Their voices were said to have carried across the valley.

The first of many songs about the Settle–Carlisle railway was composed by Mike Donald in 1970. Mike was northern area manager for E. J. Arnold & Son, the Leeds-based educational suppliers and publishers. He developed a love for folk music and set an audience laughing through his humour. He wrote, in ten minutes, what became a celebrated song about the Settle–Carlisle line. *The Dalesman*, a magazine with which I was associated, inspired Mike. I had written a book about life on the railway with David Joy, another staff member, and Mike, reading it, was inspired to compose.

The *Dalesman* eventually issued the song, and others with a Dales flavour, as an LP record. Mike had composed his song when he was returning by train from Appleby to Skipton at Christmas time in 1969. He went to great pains to ensure that the words were historically accurate. 'I just could not believe that trains were blown to a halt by gales at Ribblehead.' Confirmation was given by some old drivers with whom he chatted.

Mike's song, entitled The Settle–Carlisle Railway, began with these words and chorus:

*In the year of sixty-nine they planned to run a train—*
*From Settle to Carlisle, across the mountain range;*
*They employed three thousand navvies to build this mighty road*
*And across the fells thro' Appleby the old steam engine rolled.*

*And it's up in the morning, lads, in wind, snow or hail.*
*Hold fast to your hammers, lads, and lay another rail.*

This song, released in December 1970, led to an appearance on Border Television. His first record, a 7-inch LP, was released by the Yorkshire Dales Railway Society. Shortly afterwards, Mike wrote *Land of the Old and Grey*, a song that had a social importance; it told of young folk being forced to leave the countryside by changing economic conditions.

My old friend Dave Goulder, born on the Notts/Derby border, left school at the age of fifteen and drifted into railway work as porter, engine-cleaner, fireman, steam-raiser, tube-cleaner, and knocker-up.

Dave eventually issued an LP of melodious railway songs under the title *The Man Who Put the Engine in the Chip Shop*. His musical thoughts about the Settle–Carlisle begin with the lively words:

*The Settle–Carlisle Railway was built into the land*
*More viaducts and tunnels than the lines upon your hand*
*She cuts across the Pennines over water, rock and air*
*Seventy miles of monuments to the men who put her there.*

The chorus:

*I'd like to sit awhile, by the Settle and Carlisle*
*And delve among the memories at evening…*

Dave had a variety of jobs before he began work for the railways in 1954. He was a porter for a year, his jobs including handling parcels and releasing pigeons. He also clambered up signal posts to refuel the lamps. Dave, aged sixteen, then climbed on to the footplate of a locomotive as a fireman. His tutors in railway work were the drivers.